D1165684

Towards a High Attic

Towards a High Attic

THE EARLY LIFE OF GEORGE ELIOT

ELFRIDA VIPONT

HAMISH HAMILTON
LONDON

First published in Great Britain 1970
by Hamish Hamilton Ltd
90 Great Russell Street, London WCr
Copyright © 1970 Elfrida Vipont
Printed in Great Britain by
Western Printing Services Ltd
Bristol
SBN 241 01919 2

For
MARY LYDIA

ACKNOWLEDGEMENT

I GLADLY ACKNOWLEDGE the immense debt of gratitude I owe to the exhaustive work of George S. Haight on George Eliot, especially to his biography—*George Eliot* (Oxford University Press)—and to his complete edition of *The George Eliot Letters* (Oxford University Press), all seven volumes of which were most kindly provided for me on indefinite loan by the Librarian of the Morecambe Branch of the Lancaster County Library, Mrs Rawnsley, to whom, as always, I express my thanks.

I

THE LITTLE GIRL trailed at her brother's heels, as he raced to take up his favourite position at the window.

"Me too! Me too!" she insisted. "Wait for me, Isaac!"

"Oh, come on, Mary Ann," said seven-year-old Isaac impatiently. "You silly little thing, you'll miss it if you don't hurry!"

He had no intention of missing anything, of course. He always had to have the best place. However, he held out a helping hand to four-year-old Mary Ann as she wriggled into position beside him.

"I can hear it!" she said.

"No, you can't," he scoffed. "That's only a chaise—it isn't half loud enough. Now, *listen!*"

Mary Ann clung to him in her excitement as she listened, but he shrugged her off. He was fond of his younger sister but she would carry on so.

"*Listen!*" he repeated.

The thin, clear sound of a horn broke upon the silent air. Then came the drumming of hooves, louder, louder, tumultuously louder, until at last the mail coach hove in sight.

Mary Ann turned to Isaac. "Ooh—look!" she exclaimed, not wanting him to miss anything. "Look, Isaac!"

As if he wasn't looking! As if he couldn't see the coach perfectly well without having his attention drawn to it by Mary Ann. She would miss it herself if she didn't pay attention.

"Look for yourself, silly!" he said, and then both children squealed excitedly "Ooh—ooh—" because this was the most wonderful sight they knew and they never tired of it. The bend in the road slowed down the coach just sufficiently for them to see it in all its splendour; the four greys thundering by, the swaying vehicle packed with passengers and sagging with luggage and parcels of all shapes and sizes, the coachman skilfully handling the ribbons and the red-coated guard flourishing his horn.

"Ooh!" they repeated, and then Mary Ann sighed regretfully "Ooh!" as the coach disappeared from sight and only the far-off drumming of hooves lingered on the air. She went on gazing after it and then turned to Isaac again, but he had already lost interest. After all, there would be another mail coach passing by later in the day. There were always two, one in the morning from Birmingham to Stamford, and one in the afternoon from Stamford to Birmingham. You could be sure of that. Isaac was always very confident about the things he could be sure of. Mary Ann, on the other hand, never seemed to be very sure about anything.

"I'm going out," said Isaac.

"Me too! Me too!" insisted Mary Ann.

Isaac shrugged his shoulders. "Then you'd better not get caught," he observed. "You've torn your pinafore."

Mary Ann glanced down impatiently at her pinafore. First thing in the morning, it had been spotless and immaculate; now it was crumpled and dirty, with a three-cornered tear where she had caught it in her haste to get to the window in time to see the mail coach. She hid behind Isaac as they stole softly down the stairs and out through the door into the yard. The men in the farmyard would not scold her; they had more important things to think about than a torn pinafore and anyhow, they would always stick up for the master's "little wench".

The children wandered through into the garden and raided the currant bushes. The white fantails rose with a whirring of wings and then strutted on the roof of an outhouse, occasionally stopping to peer down at the children. Their white breasts shone in the sunshine and put to shame Mary Ann's untidy pinafore. She wiped her little hands down the front of it, leaving a tell-tale, pinkish stain.

"Oh, Mary Ann, you *are* a silly," scolded her brother.

They went through the garden and out into the fields, where the grass rose high, tangled with flowers and loud with the hum of bees. They paused beside the round pool and Isaac turned a lily pad or two, in search of lurking newts or sticklebacks.

"Some day I'll take you fishing in the canal," promised Isaac, and Mary Ann wished the day might go on for ever, and that she might never have to return to the house to explain the state of her pinafore.

Isaac and Mary Ann were the younger children of Robert and Christiana Evans of Griff House, near Nuneaton. Robert Evans was agent to Francis Parker Newdigate, who had brought him with him from his former home at Kirk Hallam in Derbyshire, when he had inherited the Newdigate estate at Arbury Hall. At first Robert and Christiana had lived at the South Farm, Arbury, but soon after Mary Ann's birth they had moved to Griff House, where there was more room for the growing family. At Griff, twin boys had been born, but they only lived ten days, and after that Christiana never regained her former health and vigour. Soon little Chrissie, her eldest child, was sent as a boarder to a small school in the neighbouring village of Attleborough and it was arranged for Isaac and Mary Ann to spend some time each day at a dame school nearby. Their sister Chrissie did not very much mind going to boarding school at such an early age; she was a docile, well-behaved little girl who always did as she was told and never dirtied her spotless pinafores. Also the school was near the home of her favourite aunt, Mrs Everard, who was very fond of her and always made much of her. "Such a *good*, well-behaved child!" she would say. "She's a regular Pearson."

Mrs Evans had been a Pearson before her marriage, and the Pearsons, in her opinion, were very important people, respectable, hard-working, and owing nothing to anybody. A Pearson could always be relied upon to do the proper thing, at the proper time, and to give advice to those less fortunate than themselves, especially if their misfortunes were their own fault. Christiana was a devoted wife and mother, and loved her husband dearly, but she never missed an opportunity of impressing upon him and the rest of the family just how important the Pearsons were. Robert Evans' first wife, Harriet, had been a domestic servant in the big house at Kirk Hallam; she too had been a devoted wife and mother, but Christiana considered that in his second marriage Robert Evans had done much better for himself. He was very fortunate, she thought, to have married a Pearson.

Robert and Harriet Evans had had three children; the youngest had died as a baby, and the others, Robert and Fanny, left home soon after Mary Ann was born. Robert was then eighteen and a very able, reliable young man; he moved to Kirk Hallam to take over his father's former job as agent, and Fanny went with him to keep house. They left home to take advantage

4

of this good opportunity, and not because they felt themselves to be in any way unwanted, for their warm-hearted stepmother had always been good to them, in spite of the undeniable fact that they were not Pearsons.

Sometimes the world seemed to Mary Ann to be veritably stiff with Pearsons. Her mother's three sisters all lived in the neighbourhood, Aunt Everard, Aunt Johnson and Aunt Garner, and all were Pearsons to their finger-tips. They would have scorned to give way to sinful pride; they knew that it was not necessary to show your pride in being a Pearson. Everybody knew that you were a Pearson and therefore, it went without saying, superior to the rest of the world. All the aunts frequently visited Griff House, sometimes singly, and sometimes on family occasions, together in a formidable group. Chrissie enjoyed these visits; neat, pretty and well-behaved, she would be singled out as a Pearson—"Bless the child, she grows more of a Pearson every day." Isaac secretly rebelled against them. He was always told how tall he was growing and what a fine lad he was, and this pleased him, but then the aunts would kiss him, Aunt Everard with a firm, decided peck, as a preliminary to asking him how he was getting on with his lessons. Isaac hated the kissing part of the business, but Mary Ann hated the whole affair. Somebody would be sure to say: "Pity the little thing's such a brown gel!" or "I'd do something about that hair if I were you, sister," or "Come, come, little gel, aren't you going to speak to your kind auntie who's come all this way a'purpose to see you!"

By no stretch of the imagination could Mary Ann be mistaken for a Pearson. Pearsons were good-looking, neat, predictable and sure of themselves; Mary Ann was plain, untidy, unpredictable and supremely unsure of herself. Of all three children, she was the least satisfactory in the eyes of the auntly inquisition.

She would peer up at them through the mop of soft brown hair which was for ever falling into her eyes, hiding her longing for their affection with a rebellious expression which heightened their disapproval. What an unaccountable little thing she was! And however would sister Evans manage to bring her up to be a credit to them?

There were at that time no visitors from the Evans side of the family. Most of them lived a long way off, or so it seemed, in Staffordshire or Derbyshire. In any case, the Evans family could not be compared with the Pearsons, for everybody knew that Robert Evans was a self-educated man. He himself made no attempt to hide the fact; he was quietly proud of the position he had won for himself. His father, George Evans, had been a carpenter who early in life had left his native Wales and migrated to the village of Roston Common, near Norbury, on the borders of Staffordshire and Derbyshire. There he had built up a good business, first as a carpenter, and then as a builder. He trained each of his five sons in succession. The fourth, Robert, was as good a worker as his father but considerably more gifted and ambitious. He soon attracted the attention of one of his father's clients, Mr Francis Parker Newdigate, who employed him as his agent. On his marriage, Robert Evans settled at Ellastone, in Staffordshire, and tried to combine helping his father with working for Mr Newdigate, but soon this proved to be impracticable, and Mr Newdigate set him up on a farm at Kirk Hallam.

Robert Evans may have been a self-educated man, but he was an expert in many fields. He understood farming and land valuation, road-making and surveying, estate management, building and forestry. It was said that he could estimate accurately the amount of timber in a standing tree. Soon he also acquired a knowledge of coal-mining; when he came to

6

Arbury, he was responsible for developing the mine under the estate and transporting the product by canal. His younger children were fascinated by the canal. As they grew older and ventured further afield, Isaac and Mary Ann would cross the road and wander through the fields to watch the heavily laden barges floating squatly on the brown water, drawn by slow-moving horses which plodded faithfully and dispiritedly along the towpath. Sometimes the bargees would wave cheerfully; sometimes they would shout rude words; sometimes there would be ragged children playing about the barge or a mother with a baby at her breast. Mary Ann thought she would like to live on a barge, because nobody would mind about her hair or her pinafores, but Isaac was sure there would not be enough to eat. Still, it would be nice to be able to fish all day.

Robert Evans never criticized Mary Ann for not being like the Pearsons, any more than he bothered about her tousled hair or her dirty pinafores. He would call her his "little wench" and stand up for her when she was being scolded. Often he would take her with him when he drove about the estate in his gig. The little thing would stand between his knees, sometimes lost as if in a day-dream and sometimes asking eager questions and listening intently to his answers. Soon he found that he could talk to her almost as if she were a grown-up. It was true she was not a Pearson, but on the whole Pearsons were not easy people to talk to, probably because they always knew best.

Mary Ann felt very safe when she was with her father, safe from harm and safe from criticism. She felt safe with Isaac too, of course. He was three years older than she was, and because he was a boy, she was sure he was as brave as a lion. They would play happily together by the hour in the garden or in the meadows; he even taught her to fish, though she hated putting the worm on the hook. She would gladly have trotted at his heels all day like a little dog, if only he had not sometimes turned on her and said he did not want her. It was so terrible, not to be wanted. Her father always wanted her.

Great tales were told of her father's physical strength and Mary Ann loved to hear them. It was said that once, when he was a young man, he had been travelling on top of a coach, and the woman sitting next to him had complained about the behaviour of the sailor sitting on the other side of her.

"Change over, ma'am!" Robert Evans had said briskly, and then, as he pushed himself into the place she had hurriedly vacated, he proceeded to take the astonished sailor by the collar and shove him down under the seat. Try as he would, the bully could not shake himself free from that iron hold and he remained there perforce for the rest of the journey.

More recently, Robert Evans had noticed two labourers idling in his rickyard.

"What are you doing, lads?" he asked.

"Waiting for Tom to come and help us shift this ladder to yon rick," they explained.

Robert Evans had given them one long, hard look, brushed them aside, and with a great heave of his powerful shoulders lifted the ladder unaided and carried it across to the rick.

The men who worked for him thought the world of him and so did his little daughter. She drank in everything he told her; stories of his boyhood, facts about the countryside, details about his work, and observations of the changes that were taking place—the workings of the mines which blackened the neighbouring villages with coal-dust, the new roads which made it possible for the mail coaches to maintain the extraordinary speed of ten or even twelve miles an hour, the new ideas which had crept in from dangerous foreign parts like France, where men thought nothing of murdering their betters

8

and setting themselves up as rulers, ideas which must be put down by the government, or old England would never be the same again.

Even as a very small child, Mary Ann seemed to take in these things and remember them. Nevertheless, she did not seem to take in much that she was taught at the dame school. She made no great effort to learn reading, writing or simple arithmetic; none of these things interested her, or so it seemed, and she was much happier playing with Isaac out of doors. In any case, nobody was particularly anxious for her to excel, and nobody was impressed by anything she could do. Sometimes she longed passionately to impress somebody. The aunts were always impressed by Chrissie's achievements; everybody seemed to be impressed by Isaac because he was a boy; why was nobody particularly impressed by Mary Ann? When one of the maids saw her perched on the piano stool and asked her if she could play a tune for her, she said of course she could, and opening the instrument dashed her little hands up and down the keyboard in fine imitation of the performers she had watched. It was none of her fault if the noise sounded peculiar; at least she had shown the maid that she could play.

In her daydreams, Mary Ann was an accomplished musician. She had been told that her birthday, November the twenty-second, was St Cecilia's Day and that St Cecilia was the patron saint of music, so of course she must be musical. Mary Ann knew very little about music and she had no desire to make pretty tinkling noises, playing five-finger exercises like Chrissie, but somehow she wanted to wrest music from that stubborn piano and she was determined to succeed. Meanwhile, she played brilliantly in daydreams, and in daydreams Isaac loved to listen and the aunts were suitably impressed. Her daydreams were a constant source of delight to her. She made up endless

9

stories of which she was the heroine, rescuing Isaac from rampaging bulls and fierce dogs. In these stories Isaac, of course, wanted no other companion; Mary Ann was as good as any boy and better than most. She could run faster than he and turn somersaults without being scolded by her mother; when they went fishing he would always put the worm on the hooks so as not to distress her, but she was the one who never failed to catch a fish. Sometimes it would be such a big fish that they could hardly carry it home. Yet in real life the only fish she ever caught was hooked without her knowledge when, left in charge of the rod, she sat at the water's edge while Isaac searched for bait.

Dream life was a transformation of real life, writ large. Mary Ann asked for nothing more than endless wanderings in field and garden with her adored brother, long talks with her father as they drove about the countryside, and the glimpse of the outer world afforded by the mail coach as it thundered past. These, together with freedom from lessons and aunts and curling rags, were her idea of paradise.

Nobody told her that it could not last for ever. Chrissie's early departure for boarding school should have warned her. Of course the boarding school was only three miles away, and Chrissie was often back in the family circle at Griff, but Chrissie's life, surely, could never have been quite the same again.

Christiana Evans had never regained her health after the birth and death of the twins. An energetic, houseproud woman, skilled in housewifery and all the multitudinous duties of a farmer's wife, she bravely fought down her increasing disabilities, but there came a point when something had to break, and that something was the family circle. Suddenly—or so it seemed to Mary Ann—the entire picture changed. Isaac, now eight years old, was packed off to a school at Foleshill, near

Coventry, and she herself was sent to join Chrissie at Attle-borough.

In vain little Mary Ann wept, stormed and protested. It seemed as if nobody could imagine what all the fuss was about. She was not being sent to strangers in a strange place, like Isaac. Yet Isaac made no commotion; he seemed only too eager for the new experience and the new surroundings.

"Just look at Isaac—*he* doesn't mind—and *you*'ll have Chrissie to look after you—what a lucky little girl you are!"

Mary Ann did not want Chrissie to look after her, though she loved her dearly. Sweet, docile Chrissie would never under-stand what had happened to her. All she wanted was Isaac, with everything going on just the same as ever. It was no consolation to her that Isaac did not mind.

2

UNTIL THE LAST minute, Mary Ann did not believe it would really happen. Surely her father would not let it happen. She watched Isaac, wild with excitement, collecting his treasures to take to school, and a strange, empty feeling grew inside her. Sometimes she would suddenly feel as if she were choking, and then she would run away and hide. Nobody noticed. She was very lucky to be going away to school at five years old. Many little girls never had a chance to go to school at all.

Robert Evans would miss his "little wench", to be sure, but Attleborough was only three miles distant and he would often be driving that way. And there would be holidays in plenty, and weekends to be spent at home. This was not the end of the world. But Mary Ann knew that it *was* the end of the world. She crept about with a stricken look on her plain, heavy-featured little face, while everybody else bustled about with armfuls of clothes, and piles of sewing, and freshly laundered pinafores with the smell of the goffering iron still on them. It could not really happen. It must not happen. But when all the boxes were packed—Chrissie's and Isaac's and Mary Ann's—Isaac was whisked away to Coventry, waving his cap until the last minute when the gig disappeared out of sight round the bend of the road, and Mary Ann still stood at the gate looking after him, her eyes blinded with tears.

Nobody could have considered it a hardship to go to Miss Latham's little school in Attleborough. It was more like a big family of sisters than a school. Chrissie loved it, and everybody there loved Chrissie. The girls thought they had never seen such a quaint little thing as Chrissie's younger sister. She was far younger than anybody else in the school, and they were all prepared to make a pet and a baby of her. It was a pity she was not pretty, like Chrissie. She hung back, unsure of her ground, and trying to hide her inward grief, and they laughed at her old-fashioned, serious look and nicknamed her "little mama".

"What a funny baby she is!" they would say. "She's more grown-up than we are!"

Everybody tried to be kind to her, but nobody guessed at her feelings, not even Chrissie. Day followed day, each one exactly alike. She worked at her lessons in a solitary way. This was not like the dame school, a dull interval to be suffered as patiently as might be before rushing away to enjoy real life again—playing in the garden with Isaac, exploring the fields and the canal bank, or watching for the mail coach to go by. This now was the real life, and on the whole lessons seemed to be the best part of it, in spite of the dull hopelessness of plodding along, far behind everybody else. It was no use trying to catch up with the others, but at least there was some satisfaction in mastering the work she was given and winning praise for her retentive memory. When winter came, however, even that satisfaction grew dim, for her brain seemed as frozen as her poor little body. The older children would cluster round the fire, holding out their hands to the warmth, not realizing that poor, awkward little Mary Ann, stiff with misery, dared not push between them and claim a place for herself. Home might be only a few

13

miles away, but as she shivered on the outskirts of the cheerful group at the fireside, seeing only the backs of her schoolfellows and excluded from the warmth they were enjoying, let alone their conversation and their laughter, she felt as if Griff were in another world, a lost world, a world where she had sat on the floor by the fire, with her head resting on her father's knee, not realizing that this indeed was heaven.

The nights were worst of all. Mary Ann could not explain this, even to Chrissie. She dared not confess that she was afraid of the dark. She had never been afraid of the dark at home, not with Isaac nearby and not with her father and mother within call. Darkness held no terrors at Griff. But here there were noises, strange inexplicable noises—eerie sounds from restless sleepers, creaks from the staircase, footsteps in the passages, and downstairs a rumble of adult conversation, rising and falling, and all too often transforming itself, as her terror mounted, into the growling of wild beasts creeping stealthily nearer and nearer to their quivering prey. Wide-eyed, she would lie staring into the darkness, hour after hour, and next day kind Miss Latham and her pupils would think what a pity it was that poor little Mary Ann Evans was so pale and un-responsive, when everybody was trying hard to make her feel happy and at home.

Mary Ann lived for the holidays. The weekend breaks were all too short, for she had barely settled down when it was time to return to school. The longer holidays were sheer bliss. The hateful school boxes were unpacked and stowed away in the attic, and she could pretend that she would never have to go back. She wished she could stay at home for the rest of her life, with the garden and the meadows to play in and Isaac as her constant companion. He usually reached home a little later than his sisters, to find Mary Ann waiting for him at the gate, hopping from one foot to another in her excitement and holding up her plain little face to be kissed. He did not mind giving her a hurried peck but he wished she would not fuss around so. He was glad his school friends were not there to see his little sister making such an exhibition of herself.

Isaac would shrug her off and she would follow him from place to place as he visited all their old haunts and looked about for his fishing tackle. Before long, almost imperceptibly, the old relationship would be restored and they would race off together across the fields and down to the canal, only somehow Mary Ann would be plagued by a vague suspicion that things were different, and the more she sensed a difference the more she insisted to herself that there had been no change. She had to do this; otherwise her whole world would crumble.

"You do love me, Isaac, don't you?"

"Yes, of course I do."

"Home's nicer than school, isn't it, Isaac?"

"I should hope so—what a silly little thing you are, Mary Ann!"

"Do you miss me when you're at school, Isaac?"

"Why should I? I wish you'd stop asking such stupid questions and leave a fellow alone for a change."

Nobody seemed to want her very much, either at home or at school. Her father would ruffle her tousled hair with his big, strong hand and call her his "little wench", but that was not the same as being somebody with whom she always came first. In the daydream stories she made up for herself, she *always* came first. There was no such thing as school, and there were no censorious aunts; as for night terrors, nobody was afraid of the dark, least of all Mary Ann.

Nobody knew about the daydream stories, not even Isaac. They formed a secure, happy, inner refuge which she kept to herself. Soon she found another refuge. Slowly, painfully, she had learned to read, and suddenly a whole new world was open to her. She began to read avidly, fighting her way from page to page. The first book of her very own she read over and over again. Given to her by her father, which made it doubly precious, it was called *The Linnet's Life*. She would pore lovingly over each woodcut in turn until she came to her favourite, a picture of the linnet feeding her brood. The little birds safe in their nest, the parent bird intent on feeding them, the detail of tree and spray and flower, all these things were familiar to her and all combined to convey a feeling of security.

There were not many books at Griff House. Neither the Evans nor the Pearson family indulged in reading to any great extent. Reading was deemed a waste of time, especially for a little girl who ought to be sewing, or knitting, or doing something to help her mother. When an old friend of the family visited the house one day, he noticed the child's utter absorption in *The Linnet's Life*.

"That is a pretty book, my dear," he said. "Let me hear you read."

He did not seem to notice her unruly hair or her untidy appearance. He only listened gravely as she read, and then asked her to show him some more of her pretty books. She hung her head because she did not want to admit that this was the only book she possessed. He did not question her further but stood for a moment looking along the low bookshelves with their meagre supply of unread books. Then he patted her cheek and went away, leaving her huddled up in her corner, speechless with shyness.

"You might have said thank you to the gentleman for taking notice of you, Mary Ann," said her mother reproachfully. "Why must you always be so awkward?"

Mary Ann said nothing but let the storm sweep over her. When the gentleman came again, she tried to evade him, but his quick eyes spied her out.

"Ah, there's my little reader," he said. "Let me see what I can find in my pocket."

She wished the floor would open and swallow her up. She wished there had been time for her to run away and hide. He was pulling something out of his pocket and Chrissie and Isaac were watching him eagerly. Their faces fell as he held it out to Mary Ann.

"Come, my dear," he said kindly. "This is for you."

It was a copy of *Æsop's Fables*. If she had been a Pearson, she would have known how to say thank you, but she was only little Mary Ann Evans, the plain one, the awkward one, and all she could do was to clasp the book in both hands as if she would never let it go and look up at him with her eyes full of tears.

After that the old gentleman would often bring her a book. She read them over and over again, and her appetite grew. Soon she was exploring the dreary bookshelves and finding unexpected treasures, including *The Pilgrim's Progress*, and a battered old book called *Joe Miller's Jest-Book*. She could not understand all the stories in the *Jest-Book* but some of them made her laugh. When she repeated them to the rest of the family, they also found them amusing. Her mother's tired face brightened, and her father smiled approval and called her his clever little wench. Obviously reading was more than just a pleasant occupation. Sometimes you could impress people as a result of your reading and insignificant Mary Ann had always longed to impress people.

There were few changes to vary the routine of home and school, of drives with her father and games with Isaac, of lessons

17

heavy with dullness and nights streaked with horror. There was, however, one quite unforgettable week. In the latter part of May 1826, Robert Evans decided to take his wife on a little trip into Staffordshire and Derbyshire to visit his relations, especially his brother William at Ellastone. He had been very close to William and he had not seen him for a long time. Suddenly he decided that his youngest daughter should come too. The child was beside herself with joy. Christiana Evans was glad to have one of the children with her; when visiting relations whom you do not know very well, the presence of a child gives confidence and provides a ready excuse for preoccupation when required.

Save through her reading, little Mary Ann knew of no other landscape than the flat, well-cultivated, somewhat featureless countryside surrounding her home. This she loved passionately, and all the more so because she had been taught by her father to look on it with a discerning eye. She knew the evidence of good farming and good stock-breeding and good forestry, and she also knew the signs of neglect. The rides in her father's gig, standing between his knees and listening to his observations, had given her even as a little child a sense of belonging, and of caring, as if what happened to this familiar landscape mattered to her intensely because she was part of it. Now she was suddenly whisked away, with what seemed to her amazing speed, to entirely different surroundings, to a region where you were never out of sight of the hills, where narrow roads wound steeply up or dropped abruptly, where rivers ran swiftly over pebbly beds, crossed by old stone bridges where you could be held up to see over the parapet and watch the fish flicker silently to and fro.

Her father had been born and brought up at Roston Common, near Norbury, but the place which impressed Mary Ann most was his second home, Ellastone, on the other side of the Dove, where Uncle William lived. It stood high up above the river, backed by the rising hills, with the church tower rising above the clustered cottages. There was something about the place which captured her imagination; no detail escaped her and the picture of it remained clear to her mind to become a background for many a daydream story.

They crossed over into Derbyshire and penetrated wild scenery with rocks piled high, where, as Robert Evans maintained, there was no good living to be got out of farming. This was the test, of course: Mary Ann quickly understood that scenery was all very well, but what really mattered was the agricultural value of the land. Beyond the romantic but unremunerative scenery lay Kirk Hallam, where her stepbrother, Robert, carried on her father's former work. Her stepsister, Fanny, soon won her heart by her warm welcome and sensitive understanding; Frances Evans was an attractive, nineteen-year-old girl, capable of holding strong opinions and equally capable of keeping them to herself.

Perhaps the most exciting experience of all was the visit to Lichfield on the way home, not necessarily because of the beauties of Lichfield, but because they spent the night at The Swan. Mary Ann treasured up every detail of her surroundings, every incident, however small, so that she might tell the whole story to Chrissie and Isaac on her return. It gave her an unaccustomed sense of importance to be staying at an inn, to arrive in the midst of a flurry of grooms and ostlers, to hear her father issuing commands about the care of his horses, to be ushered to a bedchamber and see the chambermaid's concern as her mother investigated the bed to make sure that it was clean and properly aired. Through the windows came the sounds of traffic, the typical traffic of a busy highway; the slow clop-clop of heavy draught horses and the rumbling of wheels, the brisk clattering of hooves as well-mounted horsemen cantered by, great coaches arriving and departing with a flourishing of horns, carriers' carts trundling heavily, whistling boys pushing their barrows, and fashionable phaetons and high-gigs swishing past. High above the turmoil towered the three spires of Lichfield Cathedral, and the West Front with its fantastic wealth of statuary. Little Mary Ann held her breath in wonder but she had no words with which to convey something so far beyond her comprehension. Doggedly she stored up the whole week in her memory, retaining everything, sharing only the obvious: you could not explain to Chrissie and Isaac what it felt like to see Ellastone, with the church tower riding high, or to look down into the clear waters of the Dove from the old stone bridge at Norbury, or to see the rocks piled up in awesome confusion, or to experience the incomparable wonder of Lichfield Cathedral, but you could tell them all about the relations, and the cottage at Roston where father had been born, about strange houses and unaccustomed food and friendly people, and above all about what it felt like to stay at The Swan.

3

PROBABLY IT WAS the arrival of the pony that marked the decisive and final change in the old brother-and-sister companionship. Yet at the time the unsuspecting Mary Ann had been even more ecstatic with joy than Isaac himself. Isaac, of course, did not want to give himself away. He had been longing for a pony of his own, but when his dream came true, he managed not to betray any undue emotion. If any of Mary Ann's daydreams had come true, it would have been a very different matter, but of course Isaac's imagination did not stray far beyond the realms of probability.

At first he was very magnanimous about allowing Mary Ann to ride the pony. Then, as he gained confidence, he wanted to ride further afield. It was no fun to take turns with his sister in cantering round the paddock. When he went for longer rides, Mary Ann must be left behind, and this made sense to Isaac. What did not make sense was hearing Mary Ann refer to "our pony"; it was not her pony, it was his pony and he did not hesitate to make this perfectly clear. Soon Mary Ann lost all interest in the pony; it was something which had come to divide them and to spoil the old relationship.

Driven back to her books for consolation, Mary Ann read everything she could lay hands on. One memorable day, she

21

found Chrissie deep in a book which one of the neighbours had lent to her. It had an intriguing title: *Waverley*. Chrissie had no sooner laid it aside than her little sister pounced on it. She read it eagerly, in great gulps, crouched in a corner, oblivious of her surroundings, with her hair hanging about her face. She was so carried away by the story that she lived in the world Scott had created and knew no other. Nothing else mattered. Then, long before she had reached the end, came a sudden shock. She could not find the book anywhere.

"Oh, Chrissie, have you seen *Waverley?*" she asked.

"I took it back yesterday," said Chrissie. "I'd finished it. I didn't know you were reading it."

Mary Ann said no more. Stricken by this abrupt severance from her imaginary world, she shut up like a clam. Eventually she reached a firm resolution. She might never know the end of the wonderful story, but she would at least keep what she had gained of it. It would be terrible if she were to lose all the wonder and the magic. Steadily, stolidly, in her round, childish handwriting, she began to write out the story as she remembered it, beginning with Waverley's arrival at Tully Veolan. She went on doggedly until her parents, surprised to see her so quiet and industrious, found out what her employment was. Her mother could not believe her eyes. To think of it! There was the child, as quiet as a mouse, labouring away with pen and ink and never a word to anybody!

Her father's heart smote him. "See if you can get it back again, Chrissie," he suggested. "It's a shame not to let the little wench finish it."

Soon the book was restored and Mary Ann read it from cover to cover. Secretly she made up her mind that henceforth she would read every line written by Sir Walter Scott.

Mrs Evans was at a loss to understand her little daughter.

Sometimes she hardly seemed like a child at all. She did not appear to be interested in dolls, least of all in sewing for them; she did not seem to care for pretty clothes and she hated curling rags. When she went to a children's party with Chrissie—Chrissie looking as pretty as a picture and Mary Ann so plain and awkward that her worried mother was at her wit's end as she tried to make her more presentable—she would not join in any of the games and dances but sat by herself, gloomily watching the proceedings.

"My dear, you do not seem happy," said a kind lady, approaching her. "Are you enjoying yourself?"

"No, I'm not," said Mary Ann abruptly. "I don't like to play with children, I like to talk to grown-up people."

On the other hand, when she and Isaac went off together, forgetting their differences, they were as lively as ever. When Wombwell's Circus came to Nuneaton, they walked all the way there and back to see it and chattered about it ceaselessly on their return. The sights and sounds and smells of the circus dominated their conversation until they returned to school again. Then, night after haunted night, as Mary Ann lay awake, staring into the darkness, straining her ears to hear the ominous creaks from the stairs and passages, the blaring sounds of the circus would echo in her memory and the smell of sawdust would steal upon the familiar stuffiness of the dormitory.

Mary Ann's mind was growing restive. She was tired of the narrow little circle of Miss Latham's: tired of being looked down on by the older children and tired of the humdrum life. Whether she knew it or not, she needed more to bite on. When she was transferred to Mrs Wallington's school in Nuneaton, she welcomed the change. If she must be in a boarding school, let it be a larger one, where she could really learn something and where perhaps it would not matter so much that she was plain.

Mrs Wallington was a widow and she had been running her school in Vicarage Street very successfully for some years, with the help of her daughter, Nancy. By the time Mary Ann Evans arrived in 1828, there were about thirty boarders; Nancy Wallington had left to be married and her friend, Maria Lewis, was the principal governess.

Maria Lewis looked down at little Mary Ann Evans and saw a plain, unattractive little girl, with the defiant look on her face which almost invariably shows that a child expects to be repulsed. Mary Ann looked up at Maria Lewis and was mesmerized by the most hideous squint she had ever encountered. Involuntarily, they smiled at one another; it was the beginning of a long friendship.

Maria Lewis was an avid reader and she at once began to stimulate Mary Ann's passion for reading. Christiana Evans was increasingly puzzled and dismayed when Mary Ann came home for holidays and half-holidays: such a consumption of candles, such late nights poring over books, surely this could not be natural for a little girl, especially for one with Pearson blood in her veins. Nevertheless, Mary Ann continued to devour every book which came her way, in particular every novel written by Sir Walter Scott.

An Irish woman herself, Maria Lewis had always taken great pains to speak what she felt to be correct English. She was horrified by Mary Ann's Warwickshire accent. The child was obviously clever, and might hope to teach when she grew up, for her plain, heavy looks made matrimony seem very unlikely. She could never expect to find a good post unless she got rid of that appalling accent, and so Maria Lewis set to work at once. Mary Ann was at first astonished by this; she spoke as

24

everybody else did at Griff and Attleborough, and the surrounding district, with the exception of the "quality", of course. Even the Pearson aunts used the prevailing dialect. Miss Lewis brushed protestations aside. She set to work to transform Mary Ann's country speech, but for a long time she only succeeded in making her speak in a halting, pedantic fashion, except when the child forgot herself and lapsed into dialect.

Above all, Maria Lewis was an ardent churchwoman. A new movement had been sweeping through the Church of England, and though it was late in arriving in old-fashioned Nuneaton, Maria Lewis was already strongly influenced by it. Mary Ann listened to her with astonishment. At home, churchgoing was the proper thing to do. The Evans family attended Chilvers Coton Church in their best clothes as a matter of duty; it was, of course, very important to be seen to be there. Miss Lewis seemed to think that this was not the heart of the matter at all; what mattered was not only attendance at church, but what you did and how you lived during the rest of the week, and whether you read your Bible and said your prayers regularly. Mary Ann had never heard of anybody who took religion so seriously, with the exception of her Uncle Samuel, her father's youngest brother, and his wife, Elizabeth, who had joined the Methodists. Miss Lewis would have been shocked if anybody had accused her of being influenced by Methodism; she was such a staunch member of the Church of England that she would only teach in Church of England families and schools, and had once refused to take up a very good post when she discovered that her would-be employer was a Nonconformist.

The more interest Maria Lewis took in Mary Ann Evans, the more the child responded to her. Nobody had taken such an interest in her before. The slightest encouragement from her adored brother, Isaac, had been enough to inspire her to attempt all kinds of boyish exploits and occupations in order to please him. Similarly this warm, loving encouragement from Maria Lewis called forth such affection and admiration from little Mary Ann Evans, that she was prepared to read the Bible over and over again, from cover to cover, to renounce the Devil and all his works, and to turn away from any occupation which might be considered in the least worldly or frivolous. Miss Lewis was an angel: Miss Lewis was a saint: Mary Ann's daydream stories were full of Miss Lewis, and it was she now, and not Isaac, who needed to be rescued from imaginary rampaging bulls and fierce, marauding dogs. Mary Ann would willingly have died for her.

Every Sunday the girls from Mrs Wallington's school walked the short distance to the old parish church in a demure crocodile, to the utter distraction of the boys from the neighbouring grammar school. Once safely shut up in the box pews which then filled the church, they were free to let their minds wander as they would, provided they maintained due decorum in public and restrained themselves from too obvious titters when little Mr Hughes, the curate in charge, came bustling in with his preposterous little brown wig askew. Surely nobody could be blamed for not listening to the sermon, for nobody could hear a word of what Mr Hughes said. When he mounted into the vast three-decker pulpit, set right in the middle of the chancel, facing the congregation, his discourse was almost completely inaudible. Even the adults could not resist smiling at the Reverend Hugh Hughes, though everybody liked and tolerated him. Then, suddenly, the little man was swept into the centre of a controversy which was none of his seeking. An evangelical curate, the Reverend John Edward Jones, was appointed to the new church at Stockingford and his preaching proved so popular and inspiring that people flocked to hear him. The Bishop, Henry Ryder, himself an evangelical, gave Mr Jones permission to deliver a series of evening lectures in Nuneaton Parish Church, and in almost no time the town was split into factions, some supporting the Reverend Hughes, others the Reverend Jones. Feelings ran high and at times violence was threatened. Maria Lewis supported Mr Jones, and so did her friend, Nancy Buchanan, the former Miss Wallington: Nancy's husband, on the other hand, was one of the Reverend Hughes' strongest supporters, so that even families were bitterly divided in this dispute.

None of this was lost on Mary Ann Evans. She was intensely aware of the tension in the little town and of the personalities involved. She took sides as vigorously as her teacher, but behind all this she was beginning to sense something deeper. On the face of it, one side might be right and the other wrong, but the rightness and the wrongness seemed to have very little to do with the Christian life which Miss Lewis talked about so earnestly. Only, of course, the adored one could never, in any circumstances, be wrong.

The adored one could never be wrong. Nevertheless, perhaps Mary Ann could have wished her to be wrong when she began to insist that the time had come for her twelve-year-old pupil to change schools again. If this had meant parting from Maria Lewis, Mary Ann might have rebelled, but there was no question of severing the friendship. Mr and Mrs Evans were only too thankful to have found somebody who appeared to understand their difficult daughter; they made friends with Miss Lewis, entertained her when visiting the child, and listened to her advice. Gently, inexorably, Miss Lewis managed to convince them that Mary Ann was clever. At last they knew what was the matter with her: she might be plain and unattractive and awkward, but at least she was clever. It would

27

have been much more suitable for Isaac to have been the clever member of the family.

Maria Lewis had very little difficulty in persuading Mary Ann's parents to send her to an even better school.

"We have been able to do well for her so far here," she explained. "But now there is nothing more we can teach her. She has a quite exceptional brain."

In an obscure way, Robert Evans had always pinned his faith on his "little wench". Chrissie and Isaac were Pearsons at heart; he loved them dearly but both had, and would always have, that subtly superior touch which comes of knowing how well you become that station in life to which you know God has called you. Mary Ann was sure of nothing. Even her evangelical fervour was a mask, just as her tomboyish phase had been a mask. Behind the mask was a child supremely unsure of anything. Unaware of any station in life to which it might be supposed that God had called her, hungry for notice, an ugly duckling with no hope of turning into a swan, Mary Ann Evans was yet becoming dimly conscious that she had latent within her powers which would stifle her if she could not learn to use them, but for which the world in which she had been born and brought up, the world to which she was passionately attached, the world in which, so far as she could see, her future would inevitably lie, had no possible outlet, no possible manner of use.

4

ONCE AGAIN, Mary Ann Evans was thrust into a new world. This time, however, she was at least in some degree armed to meet the situation. She knew now that she was clever, and that her cleverness had won for her the opportunities offered by an education at the Miss Franklins' school in Coventry. Families who were ambitious for their daughters were willing to send them hundreds of miles to be educated by the Miss Franklins. One girl came from India, another from New York, others from many parts of England, including London, where one would have thought there were good schools in plenty for young ladies. Torn from her adored Miss Lewis, severed yet further from her well-loved home, Mary Ann found her feet more easily than she could possibly have anticipated, for there was something in the atmosphere of this school which suited her. The Miss Franklins knew that she was exceptionally gifted and they expected her to do them credit; the girls accepted her without fuss; the lessons opened up a new world for her. It was a world in which she felt at home.

In an age when dancing and deportment were considered to be of more importance in female education than literature and mathematics, the Miss Franklins offered quite exceptional advantages to the girls in their charge. Miss Mary Franklin was the eldest daughter of the Rev. Francis Franklin, for many years a well-known Baptist minister in Coventry. Everybody knew "Grandpa Franklin", a little man with a big head and a kind heart, and an upsetting habit of expecting the children who attended his little chapel in Cow Lane to remember the texts of his sermons. Miss Franklin had started the school in the family home. She was an excellent teacher and a good business woman, and the number of pupils increased. Her younger sister, Miss Rebecca, had enjoyed the advantage of a year's schooling in Paris; she was considered to be an authority on deportment, and correct etiquette, and good taste in literature, and the girls were encouraged to copy her style in conversation and correspondence. Mary Ann Evans met this new challenge with enthusiasm; the letters in which she shared her feelings and experiences with Miss Lewis rapidly became studied, formal and painstaking, until they were more like the effusions of a mediocre eighteenth-century essayist than the outpourings of a young nineteenth-century schoolgirl.

By the time Mary Ann Evans arrived as a new girl, in 1832, the school had long outgrown the little Franklin home in Cow Lane. Already it had moved twice, and it was now established in a big, roomy house in Warwick Row. The girls were taught English and Arithmetic, History and French, Music and Drawing, and great attention was paid to neat handwriting, good manners, and correct pronunciation. Miss Rebecca's concern was quickly aroused by Mary Ann's Warwickshire accent; though she no longer spoke in the broad dialect which Miss Lewis had taken such pains to correct, she still used many country expressions and turns of phrase—as Shakespeare probably did before her. Miss Rebecca would have none of this. She carefully drilled her willing pupil until Mary Ann's speech resembled her own—correct, stilted, slightly pompous, with no trace of the earthy, pithy way of speech characteristic of rural England. Fortunately it is possible to be bi-lingual; most children who are trained to forgo their native dialect can revert to it at will.

Some of the girls who came from a distance envied Mary Ann for being so near her home. Every week her father would send a supply of new-laid eggs and other farm produce, and often he would call to see her when some business errand brought him to Coventry. It was a pity Isaac was no longer at Foleshill; he had outgrown his first school and was studying under a tutor in Birmingham. They met, of course, in the holidays, but the old bond between them seemed to be growing weaker. Isaac was a cheerful youth with a very conventional outlook on life. He liked always to do the correct thing, which included attendance at church on Sunday mornings, but he disliked intensely anything which might make him feel conspicuous. His younger sister's enthusiasm, and especially her evangelical fervour, seemed to him quite immoderate and foolish; the sensible thing in life was to do what convention required of you and enjoy yourself for the rest of the time.

Isaac shared his father's views on politics. He was all against the introduction of new-fangled notions. The old order was best, the aristocracy and the "quality" were the only people fitted to hold authority, revolutionary ideas were taboo, and all reformers ought to be put down, or at the very least held up to ridicule. Far too many people in the evangelical movement were tainted with a reforming spirit, and Isaac would have none of them.

The passing of the Reform Bill in 1832, for the reform of the franchise, brought consternation to Griff. Robert Evans

31

prophesied disaster and his son heartily agreed with him. What the country needed was not reform, but strong government in the old tradition, and no quarter for the Radicals. Yet here was this preposterous Bill which did away with perfectly respectable institutions, like rotten boroughs and the right of certain landowners to nominate members of parliament, so as to give representation to upstart places like Manchester, Leeds, Sheffield, and Birmingham, and which extended the vote to any Tom, Dick or Harry of a shopkeeper or tenant farmer with a rateable value of £10 a year. This would lead to anarchy, prophesied Robert and Isaac Evans, and the election riots at Nuneaton later in the year strengthened them in their conviction.

Mary Ann actually witnessed the election riots, for they occurred shortly after her thirteenth birthday, early in the Christmas vacation, when she was spending a few days with Miss Lewis. There was no question, naturally, of venturing near the polling booths. Trouble was confidently expected and Miss Lewis was well aware of her responsibilities with regard to her guest.

"We shall have to spend our time quietly indoors, my dear," she said firmly. "I am told the streets will hardly be safe for respectable females."

Mary Ann was determined to see what she could. She knew, of course, that the reason for any undue disturbances at the election would be the iniquitous Reform Bill. Her father had explained to her many times how dangerous it was to extend the franchise. Unscrupulous agitators would rouse up the mob to intimidate these new and probably nervous voters, who could easily be swayed this way or that; the aristocracy and the gentry were the only people who understood the business of politics sufficiently to cast their votes, and it was to be hoped

32

they would not be so sickened by the crude behaviour of their inferiors as to retire altogether from the political scene and inflict irreparable loss upon their ungrateful country. The situation was all very simple when her father explained it to her. Nevertheless, she was curious about it.

The election was to start early in the morning on December the twenty-first, and long before dawn it was obvious that something unusual was toward. As Mary Ann lay in bed she could hear the tramping of feet through the darkness and the clatter of horses' hooves.

"Did you ever hear such a noise?" inquired Miss Lewis at the breakfast table. "It's even worse than the fair."

"But surely *all* those men can't be going to vote," said Mary Ann.

Miss Lewis shook her head. "Oh, no, no, those sorts of people are not allowed to vote," she replied, pursing her lips rather grimly at the very idea of associating navvies and colliers and labourers with the right to govern the country.

Sensible people went early to the polling booths but even they, so it was reported, were finding the experience unpleasant. Increasing crowds were lining the route and amusing themselves by jeering at the voters, especially at those who were known to be Tories. So far they were good-humoured, but as drinks were being freely distributed, it was questionable for how long they would remain so. By midday, voters were being prevented from reaching the polling booths; they were jostled and threatened and sworn at for dirty Tories. The mob was in an ugly mood and at last the magistrates decided to send for a detachment of the Scots Greys to keep order in the streets. Even the reading of the Riot Act from the window of the Newdigate Arms failed to bring people to their senses; the mob continued defiant, shouting threats and hurling missiles

33

until the whole town was in an uproar. Maria Lewis and Mary Ann Evans, watching anxiously from a window, heard that kind, pleasant Colonel Newdigate, Francis Newdigate's son, had been injured. What a shock for Robert Evans, who loved and served the Newdigate family and regarded them and others like them as England's bulwarks against anarchy and revolution!

The second day was even worse, with the Scots Greys struggling to maintain order and the drunken mob rioting in the streets. Shopkeepers barricaded their premises and householders barred their doors. Would-be voters stayed on the outskirts of the town, appealing for protection; and even those who were escorted by the military did not escape violence. Some were threatened and punched, some were beaten, and others literally had the clothes torn off their backs. Before order could be restored there was a toll of serious injuries and one death, which seemed to Robert Evans a terrible price to pay for reforms which no decent citizen could possibly want and which would be the ruin of the country. Mary Ann made few comments but her keen eyes and ears had taken in every detail. She stored the whole scene away in the back of her mind, together with some disturbing questions about the world and politics, and the men who stirred up riots—as distinct from the people actually involved in them.

Mary Ann did not go so far as to question her brother's views on politics, but increasingly she tried to interfere with his religious beliefs. Unfortunately, she felt this was her sacred duty. Under Maria Lewis's influence, she had begun to take religion very seriously indeed and now, at Miss Franklin's school, she was in an atmosphere where it mattered intensely whether you were "saved", and whether you were trying to

34

"save" others. Miss Lewis's was a gentle faith; she was persuasive rather than forceful. She had encouraged Mary Ann to study the Bible and live by its precepts, to attend church regularly and listen attentively to the sermon, to do good by helping the sick and the needy. Here was something more militant. Here were the dangers of hell fire and damnation, and the absolute necessity for conversion.

Still open to the influence of anybody who would love her and take an interest in her, Mary Ann plunged with enthusiasm into this harsher interpretation of Christianity. She did not join the Baptist Church, but she attended the Rev. Francis Franklin's chapel in Cow Lane every Sunday with the other girls, and was one of their leaders in the regular prayer meetings they held during the week. Most of them were completely won over by Dr Franklin's preaching, and intensely aware of the constant need for watchfulness if they were to be sure of salvation. Mary Ann could not see the slightest sign of such awareness in her brother, Isaac. All she could see was an indulgence in worldly pleasures which he considered to be well paid for by regular attendance at Chilvers Coton Church on Sunday mornings.

The brother and sister were growing further and further apart. From Isaac's point of view, what could be more innocent than the pleasures he enjoyed? It was not as if he went about rolling drunk, like some of the fellows he knew, or squandered his father's well-earned money at the gaming table or on horse-racing. He conceived himself to be a thoroughly respectable young man, free from vicious habits, and the last thing he wanted was to be followed round by a lugubrious sister intent on "saving" him. Besides, the more fervent she was, the more freakish she became. As a little girl she had been untidy in her appearance; now she was dowdy and, in his opinion, inexpressibly dreary. He shrugged her aside with increasing impatience and insisted on going his own way. The more he insisted, the more frantic with anxiety his sister became, for she was convinced that her darling brother was going to perdition.

Apart from their religious fervour, the pupils at the Miss Franklins' school were very normal schoolgirls for their day. They were made to work hard and they were encouraged to read widely, but in their spare time they sighed sentimentally over the mawkish verses in the popular albums which were all the rage, and copied them out carefully in their notebooks. Everything, of course, went into their notebooks. Problems of arithmetic were first worked out there, and then transcribed with meticulous care into their arithmetic books, which were later taken home to astonish their proud parents. English compositions, in the stiff eighteenth-century style favoured by Miss Rebecca, were first written down there, often with alternative words or sentences to be pondered over before a final version was approved. On the other hand, the verses were for their private enjoyment alone. The more sentimental they were, the more enthusiastically the girls hastened to copy them out; they loved verses about forsaken maidens, false lovers and early deaths.

Mary Ann was no exception to the rule. Nobody, so far, had instilled into her any sense of poetic values, and she took her standards ready-made from the other girls. She had an idea that she could easily write poetry herself, if she tried. There did not seem to be much difficulty about it, so long as you knew enough rhymes. She seldom completed her efforts, however; somehow she lost interest. She tried her hand at a story, but she did not finish that either. She still loved historical novels, and devoured tale after tale by Scott and Bulwer

Lytton, and Scott's prolific imitator, G. P. R. James. Soon she decided to write one herself, about romantic castles and star-crossed lovers and stern, unyielding relations. She ploughed industriously through seven tightly-packed pages, but then gave up the attempt. There seemed to be more pitfalls than she had thought possible.

With English composition, things were very different. Mary Ann quickly established herself as Miss Rebecca's star pupil. "Faultless, dear sister, faultless!" Miss Rebecca would say to Miss Franklin, and they would read the little essays aloud in the privacy of their own parlour, making no attempt at correction. The other girls were soon made to feel that they could not hope to reach the high standard set by Mary Ann Evans.

Mary Ann enjoyed writing compositions for Miss Rebecca, partly because she could be sure of the warmth of her teacher's approval, and partly because she found a great deal of satisfaction in tackling a job she knew she could do well. They were purely formal exercises, of course. There was nothing personal revealed in them, and Miss Rebecca would have been shocked if her pupil had erred in that direction. It was not ladylike to betray your feelings. Very occasionally, however, Miss Rebecca could have found out a good deal about Mary Ann Evans if she had cared to read between the lines. For instance, there was the subject of *Affectation and Conceit*, which on the face of it seemed to call for nothing more than the usual trite imitation of eighteenth-century essayists. Nevertheless, Mary Ann pounced on it.

The plain, awkward child had grown into a plain, awkward girl. She could not even make the best of herself, for she had no interest in dress and not an atom of charm. Thus she had always chafed subconsciously against a feeling of inferiority, first to Chrissie, dearly as she loved her, and then to her prettier schoolfellows. Given a subject after her own heart, she could hardly wait to say what she thought about conceited people, however much she might assure herself that she had no particular person in mind. She wrote: "The women guilty of this foible, are those who set great store by their personal charms these in their youth they consider sufficient to secure the admiration and worship of the whole world and safe in this belief they flutter on the flattered of the one sex, the envy of the other; and they are happy while thus admired and envied, their whole minds being in one confusion and whirl of excitement and vanity; They study no graces of mind or intellect their whole thoughts are how they shall best maintain their empire over their surrounding inferiors, and the right fit of a dress or bonnet will occupy their minds for hours together."

Earlier in the essay she wrote: "The conceited man is vain of some superiority over his fellows which he is falsely conscious of possessing." This was the rub, of course. This was where the shoe pinched. Mary Ann Evans stubbornly refused to accept the superiority of good looks or social graces. Like the rebellious little girl who had glowered through her tousled hair at the Pearson aunts, she was determined to stand her ground.

In the way of many schoolgirls, Mary Ann often started her notebooks first at one end, and then at the other, signing them at both ends so that anybody picking one up casually would have no doubt as to the identity of the owner. Sometimes she would amuse herself by varying the spelling. Mary Ann was rather a plain name, she thought; what a pity her parents had not chosen something more fashionable—Marianne was coming into fashion and that, surely, was much prettier, whether you pronounced it in the French way, or in the current English manner, "Mary-anna", or as Marian, which on the whole she preferred. Some day, perhaps, she might please herself and adapt her name as she wished, but meanwhile she contented herself with signing her notebooks "Marianne Evans". Occasionally, she was nicknamed "Polly".

On the whole, the girls were fond of Mary Ann Evans and some of them became her close friends, especially a local girl called Martha or "Patty" Jackson, and a girl from London called Jessie Barclay. Nevertheless, most of the girls felt a little shy of her, because of her reputation for learning. Her compositions, always admired by their teachers, her swift mastery of French, her prowess in music, all impressed her fellow pupils. The music-master, bored with teaching girls who did not want to learn, thoroughly enjoyed the lessons he gave to this strange girl who so yearned to excel. After some time, he even suggested that there was little more he could teach her, and the pupils who were stuck on scales and five-finger exercises, were suitably impressed.

They liked her, but in a curious way they felt separated from her. It was not only because of her cleverness; on the whole they were rather proud of having such a clever girl in the school, and obviously the poor thing needed some compensation for being so very plain. But she had such a grown-up manner and spoke in such a stiff, correct way—"My dear," said one of the pretty girls. "Do you think she was *ever* like us? I mean, I can't imagine her as a baby, can you?"

One day the bell rang and the maid who answered it ushered a visitor into the parlour and went off to find the Miss Franklins. Meanwhile Mary Ann came in with a book in her hand, intending to return it to its place on the book-shelves.

On seeing the visitor, Mary Ann started, and then addressed her in her polite, polished manner. "I beg your pardon, Ma'am," she said. "I trust I have not disturbed you."

The visitor rose from her seat. "Miss Rebecca Franklin, I presume?" she said.

There was a titter from behind the door, as one of her schoolfellows overheard her.

"Girls! Girls!" she exclaimed, as she rushed into the school-room. "What *do* you think? There's a lady in the parlour and she has mistaken Mary Ann for Miss Rebecca!"

By the time Mary Ann rejoined them, in some confusion, they had managed to suppress their giggles. Some of them cast her pitying glances. How could they have borne it if it had happened to one of them? But then, of course, no other girl in the school could possibly have been mistaken for that re-doubtable lady.

The girls were all the more astonished when they found chinks in Mary Ann's armour. Sometimes they were at a loss to understand her reactions. She would be called to play the piano before important visitors and she would give what seemed to all a brilliant performance for a mere schoolgirl, but as soon as the door of the parlour closed behind her, she would rush away to her room and burst into tears. Her com-panions were mystified by such behaviour. Could she be showing off? Or was she really upset? They did not know whether to sympathize with her or leave her alone. Then one of them made an astonishing discovery. Opening a dictionary by chance, she noticed a poem written on the fly-leaf. There was nothing strange about this, of course. The girls were always copying out their favourite poems. She glanced at it

40

curiously, to see which poem this particular girl had chosen. Too late she discovered that it was not intended for her eyes. It was an original poem and she recognized the handwriting. It had been written by Mary Ann, and it was a passionate plea for love.

5

MARY ANN's schooldays ended abruptly. She left at the end of the winter term, just before her sixteenth birthday, and went home to help Chrissie to nurse their mother. Christiana Evans' ill health had increased, at first steadily, and then rapidly, and now she was dying of cancer. Shortly after Mary Ann's return, Robert Evans too was stricken, suffering terribly from severe attacks of pain caused by stones in the kidneys. He gradually recovered, but he never regained his former health and strength. His wife died, nursed devotedly by her two young daughters, and so ended the old régime of Griff House, which had been the background of Mary Ann's life ever since she could remember.

There were, of course, a few months that just had to be lived through. The strain of her mother's illness, the shock of the realization that only in death could she find relief from pain, the anxiety for her father and the relief of his slow return to life, all combined to create a gulf between her present life and the world of school.

For some time Chrissie and Mary Ann were mercifully kept busy with the running of the house and the dairy, with entertaining visitors, looking after their father and brother, mending, sewing, and coping with all the multitudinous jobs of a busy farming household. Mary Ann found some relief to her feelings in caring for her father. The special relationship between them now provided the one element of stability in her life. After a while, it became obvious that Chrissie would not be sharing the responsibility for Griff House with her for much longer. Chrissie Evans and Edmund Clarke, a young doctor with a practice at Meriden, about five miles from Coventry, had fallen most happily in love. They were married at Chilvers Coton Church on the thirteenth of May, 1837, and Mary Ann was bridesmaid. Henceforth she was to be the sole mistress of Griff.

Robert Evans was still anxious to do his best for this youngest child of his. He had a vague idea that her education had been cut short, and he was anxious to make amends. He still stood rather in awe of that remarkable brain discovered by Maria Lewis, and though this kind of thing in a woman was something of which he had no experience, and which, in fact, he could not understand, he was determined to do what he could for this awkward phenomenon of a daughter. During the next few years, masters came from Coventry to help her with her studies. She learned Italian, German and music, and she began to teach herself Latin. She also read incessantly, tackling all manner of religious books with evangelical zeal and also wallowing in novels, biographies, essays and poetry.

Mary Ann's life was becoming a ceaseless round of activity. Behind it all, there was a constant self-questioning as to what on earth it was all about, but the more she wondered, the more she threw herself into her routine of housewifely duties. This, apparently, was a woman's work in the world, and she would excel in it as she had excelled in every other task to which she

43

had set her hand—except the obvious one of making herself attractive to other people, especially to those of the opposite sex. She took pride in pursuing her studies without detriment to her housewifery, and stored up information in her retentive brain as if she could satisfy her hungry intellect by choking it with knowledge. When the latent powers within her felt starved for lack of outlet, she flew to her religion and found such consolation as she could. With restless energy, she plunged into good works—sick visiting and charitable work amongst the poor of the neighbourhood—but even these did not satisfy her religious promptings. It was as if her evangelical zeal had turned sour on itself, until all the things she most enjoyed became open to question. Was it right to read novels—fanciful stories about things which had never happened? Even her childish daydreams had only been castles in the air; was it right to muse on things which had no real existence? Increasingly she tortured herself and poured out her feelings in long letters to Maria Lewis, who was now a private governess in Burton Latimer, Northamptonshire, having left the school at Nuneaton for reasons of health.

Isaac, still the adored brother, had the bright idea of taking her to London for a week's holiday in the summer of 1838. He was a gay though hard-working young man, and knew his way about town. Surely it would do this solemn sister of his good to see the sights of London and enjoy herself for a change! They set off together very happily by coach. Isaac was in high spirits, and Mary Ann was looking forward to spending a whole week in her brother's sole companionship. It seemed a long time since the days when they used to watch the coaches go by from the window at Griff. "Me too! Me too!" the little sister had clamoured, and the older brother, like a magnanimous god, had made room for her at his side. Could one ever recapture a perfect relationship? Sometimes it seemed to Mary Ann as if the golden gates of childhood had closed behind them, never to be opened more.

At first the scenery was familiar. They passed through little coal-blackened towns, and down narrow village streets where the cottages shook with the looms of the weavers, and through acre after acre of the well-cultivated farmland which, in Robert Evans' opinion, constituted the best scenery in England. Then they came to rolling uplands where great flocks of sheep grazed under the watchful eye of the shepherd with his dog at heel, and so again to rich farming country and prosperous market towns. As they approached a scheduled stop, the guard would blow his horn so that the innkeeper might bustle up his staff to have a meal ready on the table. Everybody would alight in a hurry, and Isaac would urge Mary Ann to be quick and waste no time, otherwise they might go hungry. Isaac was a very normal young man and he had no intention of missing his meal, as many coach travellers had to do.

"Time's up, ladies and gentlemen—can't wait—must go!" the guard would shout, when they had only swallowed a few mouthfuls. "Time's up! Time's up!"

Mary Ann would push away her plate in a panic, and Isaac would dive for another chop or a mouthful of beef, and off they would go, grumbling at the rogues who took their money for a meal and would not allow them time to eat it.

At last they clattered into London, with the horses all in a lather of sweat after the final burst of speed which ensured the prompt arrival of the coach. Isaac took command of the situation, brushing aside touts and beggars, demanding their luggage, and finally conducting his sister to the inn of his choice where he installed her in a comfortable room and made sure her wants were supplied. Could a brother do more? He did not

45

even expect very much in return; he only wanted her to enjoy herself.

In the event, nothing could have been more disappointing. Mary Ann thought very little of "the stir of the great Babel", as she called it, grimly quoting Cowper. She gloomed round the sights, but was not impressed by them; on the whole, she liked Greenwich Hospital best, but she made it quite clear to Isaac that she regarded sight-seeing as work rather than pleasure, and that her mind was on higher things. When he took her shopping, all she wanted to buy was Josephus's *History of the Jews*, and he could only relieve his feelings by buying a couple of sporting prints for himself at the same shop.

"Let's go to the theatre," he suggested on their first evening. "What would you like best to see?"

"How can you suggest such a thing, Isaac dear?" she asked him in shocked tones. "Surely you cannot regard the theatre as a suitable resort for a sincere Christian?"

"I don't know what you mean, Polly," he protested. "I'm as good a Christian as you are, and *I'm* going."

"Then I shall stay here in my comfortable bedroom and read," she declared, and nothing would move her.

Every evening Isaac breezed off to the theatre, and every evening Mary Ann sat solemnly in her bedroom and read Josephus's *History of the Jews*. Even when he did his best to please her by taking her to a service at St Paul's Cathedral, she was shocked by the behaviour she observed in the choir stalls, and he had to be satisfied with her sober assurance that she liked the mellow sound of the great bell better than anything she had heard in London so far. On the whole, Isaac was glad when the week was over.

Mary Ann, too, was glad to be back at Griff. London was indeed a "great Babel", where temptation abounded, and a

46

sincere Christian could find no peace and little enjoyment. The prospect of a visit to the Miss Franklins at Coventry seemed more promising. Nobody could take religion more seriously than the daughters of the Rev. Francis Franklin, and in their hospitable home even the most sincere Christian might rightly look forward to an experience of unalloyed happiness. Happiness seemed so simple and natural for other people; Isaac, for example, took it for granted. But for Mary Ann, at war within herself, there were endless doubts and difficulties to be overcome. At Coventry, with the devout Miss Franklins, she could at least enjoy a little respite.

The visit began happily, for the Miss Franklins spared no effort in entertaining their gifted pupil. However, on the last day Miss Rebecca took her to a musical performance at St Michael's Church (later the cathedral), which had been arranged in honour of her former music master, who was the church organist. This concert would surely offer a rare treat to Mary Ann Evans, for there was nothing of the kind to be enjoyed in Nuneaton. The exceptionally full programme included Haydn's *Creation*, Handel's *Jephtha*, and Mendelssohn's *Paul*, which was the popular composer's most recent work. Some of the finest singers of the day had been engaged and a memorable performance was assured. Yet the more Mary Ann revelled in the music, the more she tortured herself with doubts. Was it right for her to enjoy anything so much? Was it right for the singers to devote so much time and energy to perfecting themselves in their art? Ought sacred words to be used to exhibit the vocal powers of people who might not themselves be believers? The more rapturously Miss Rebecca enjoyed herself, the more reserved her companion became.

After her return, long letters sped to Martha Jackson and Maria Lewis. With Martha, she tried to argue the whole thing

47

out. She asked her if it was "consistent with millennial holiness" for singers to undergo the rigorous training which alone enabled them to develop their vocal powers. It was true that only by such training and by constant practice could their voices attain perfection, but even this perfection had human limitations and might imperil the soul. "By once admitting such reasoning," she wrote, "we disarm ourselves against opera, dancing, horse racing, nay, even against intemperance itself, which I have heard justified on the plea that since Providence has sent luxuries we are condemning them by abstinence."

It seemed as if Mary Ann could no longer enjoy music for its own sake. Not long afterwards, she wrote to Maria Lewis: "It would not cause me any regrets if the only music heard in our land were that of strict worship."

Other pleasures were laid aside almost before they had been tasted. She went to a party which must surely have delighted her brother Isaac, for the entertainment consisted entirely of dancing. Probably the conviction soon grew on her that she was a fish out of water, with her awkward manners and her unbecoming clothes, but she would not admit this even to herself. The dance music gave her a headache, and the noise and the laughter unnerved her, until at last she gave way to hysteria and retreated in floods of tears. Obviously dancing was not a suitable recreation for a sincere Christian: she had been wrong in accepting the invitation and she was resolved never to accept another.

Early in 1839, Elizabeth Evans came for the first time to stay at Griff House. She had been ill, and her brother-in-law knew well that in asking her to visit them he would please his devoted daughter. Elizabeth Evans and her husband, Samuel, were both devout Methodists, but Elizabeth was by far the better known. In her youth she had made a name for herself as an open-air preacher. A tiny, dark-eyed, indomitable young woman, she had walked miles across the country to preach the gospel on village greens and commons. Her vigorous pleadings could wean the sinner from his nefarious ways and woo the drunkard from the alehouse, and there was something about her radiant faith which gave hope to the poor and downhearted. She had ceased to preach in public when the Methodist Church began to reject the ministry of women, but she was still a powerful influence in many lives, including that of her niece Mary Ann, with whom she frequently corresponded.

Aunt Elizabeth was a visitor after Mary Ann's own heart. They could read the Bible together, pray together, and discuss religion together, and it seemed as if some of her restlessness was assuaged.

One day, as aunt and niece were sitting quietly together, Elizabeth Evans fell into a mood of reminiscence and began to relate an experience of her younger days. The story was already part of the family tradition, but now, for the first time, Mary Ann heard it complete and at first hand. The noises from the farmyard and the highway seemed to fade away as the ageing woman, her fiery eyes half closed, looked back into the past. She had been told that a young girl was to be hanged for murdering her baby and that she had refused to confess. This seemed to Elizabeth a direct challenge. To die unrepentant was to court hellfire, and surely it was her Christian duty to save this erring soul at the eleventh hour. She hastened to the gaol where she found the poor young thing crouching miserably in a corner, refusing to speak to anybody. Her urgent pleadings evoked no response whatever; the girl looked at her dumbly and said not a word. For the first time Elizabeth felt utterly helpless, utterly useless, and at the end of her resources. At last she stopped trying to persuade the girl and simply prayed to God for help. All night she prayed, and all night the girl maintained her stubborn silence, until at last Elizabeth felt such an overwhelming love for the girl, and for the murdered baby, that it was as if they had all been caught up together in the love of God. As dawn approached, their eyes met at last, and suddenly the girl broke down and confessed. Elizabeth stayed with her to the end. She prayed with her; she lovingly assured her of God's forgiveness; she rode with her in the cart to the place of execution, shielding her and upholding her, until there was nothing left but an overwhelming sense of the divine compassion—that "Mercy, Pity, Peace and Love" which for William Blake meant "God, our Father dear".

Elizabeth Evans may have been a fanatic in her youth, but she had reached a place of inward peace through the depth of her own experience. Mary Ann, on the other hand, had all the harshness of the recently-converted. There were times when even this favourite aunt could jar on her nerves. After three weeks, her Uncle Samuel joined them with the purpose of taking his beloved wife home again. They all sat chatting in the parlour, and Robert and Samuel found much enjoyment in recalling personalities they had known. In the course of the conversation Samuel referred to a worthy minister who had done much good, and been greatly loved, but who in a time of stress had taken to secret tippling.

"But I trust the good man is in heaven for all that," said Samuel Evans confidently.

"Oh yes," agreed his wife, with a devoutly sympathetic groan, "Oh yes–praise God!—he's in heaven—that's sure!"

Mary Ann was horrified and shocked. Were the righteous to have no compensation, then? What would be the use of maintaining your rigorous standards if weaker brethren who gave way to secret sins were to be admitted to the joys of heaven?

It seemed as if Mary Ann Evans, the devoted daughter, the learned young lady, the admirable dispenser of charity, could find no peace within herself. Outwardly, life at Griff was peaceful enough. Everything continued exactly as it had done when Christiana Evans was in control. The routine of house and dairy went on as before; butter, cheese and preserves were made; rural and family feasts and celebrations were catered for in a way with which not even a Pearson aunt could find fault; Robert Evans was scrupulously turned out, his linen freshly laundered, his garments mended, cleaned and pressed; nothing was lacking except for any sign of high spirits in the young mistress of the house, high spirits which might surely have been looked for in a girl of nineteen who apparently had everything she could possibly want, and had only to ask if she wanted more.

Mary Ann at least found some satisfaction in keeping Griff unchanged, yet changes were coming to disturb the peace of the countryside she loved so dearly. The mail coach could still be seen from the windows of Griff House, but its days were numbered. The railways were coming, and with them the decay of the roads and the canals. Mary Ann, desperate for a purpose in life, took note of these things and stored away in the back of her mind clear pictures of rural life as she had known it, and as it might never be again. Later in the year she actually travelled by rail, for her father, wishing her to enjoy a little change, took her with him on one of his business journeys and left her in London, to spend a few days with her school friend, Jessie Barclay. Travel was to be transformed in a decade, and no doubt this might affect the life of many a gifted country girl, chafing in isolation, but not surely the life of Mary Ann Evans, tied to her father and to her household duties.

At last, in the turmoil of her mind, she began to discover a few possible outlets. She tried applying herself to poetry and, working hard, produced painstaking verses. Some of these she sent to Maria Lewis, with a note suggesting that "my attempt at poetry will serve to amuse you, if no more". Sensitive to criticism, she tried to forestall it. The verses were not intended to amuse; they haltingly conveyed a feeling of depression experienced during a lonely evening walk.

> As o'er the fields by evening's light I stray,
> I hear a still, small whisper—"Come away!
> Thou must to this bright, lovely world soon say
>   Farewell!"
>
> The mandate I'll obey, my lamp prepare,
> Gird up my garments, give my soul to pray'r,
> And say to earth and all that breathe earth's air
>   "Farewell!"
>
> Thou sun, to whose parental beam I owe
> All that has gladden'd me while here below, —
> Moon, stars, and covenant confirming bow,
>   Farewell!
>
> Ye verdant meads, fair blossoms, stately trees,
> Sweet song of birds, and soothing hum of bees,
> Refreshing odours, wafted on the breeze,
>   Farewell!

When she reached the eighth verse, Mary Ann's farewell to her books was revealing; here her religious enthusiasm had never been allowed to limit her enjoyment.

Books that have been to me as chests of gold,
Which, miser like, I secretly have told,
And for them love, health, friendship, peace have sold,
Farewell!

The theme was clumsily sustained through ten laboured verses. However, Maria Lewis admired them unstintingly and soon persuaded Mary Ann to try her luck with a wider public. Eventually the poem was published in the *Christian Observer*, signed with the initials M.A.E. For the first time, Mary Ann Evans saw her own work in print.

It was not long before she had a much more ambitious project in hand. It seemed to her that many of her problems would be solved if only she could turn her studies to account in some way. She conceived the idea of working on an Ecclesiastical Chart, which would give "a chronological view of Ecclesiastical history". Soon she could see the whole thing in her mind's eye: a chart, divided up into columns, giving names and dates of Roman Emperors, historical events in church history and Jewish history, "the chronology of the Apostolical and Patristical writings, schisms and heresies"— the idea grew as she pondered over it and gradually the shape of it became clear. At last there was a sense of direction in her studies and she set to work eagerly, borrowing books from the library at Arbury Hall, and discussing the idea in correspondence with her friends. Here, surely, was something which was needed and which could be published usefully and profitably. The publication would not be entirely for her own benefit; she planned to use the profits to help build the new church at Attleborough. The whole project gave her a feeling of release, and the harder she worked on it, the stronger this feeling of release became.

Inevitably, this activity brought about a lightening of spirit, and with it, a slight change of outlook. She did not acknowledge this, even to her closest friends; she professed as fervent an evangelical faith as before; nevertheless a little fresh air began to seep into her studies. She read even more widely and began to revel in poetry, especially the poetry of Wordsworth. She also dabbled in science, and because her clear mind could not stop at dabbling, she settled down to study more deeply in certain branches—mathematics, chemistry, metaphysics and geology among them. Above all, her faculty of criticism was growing.

In May, 1840, came a sudden shock. She found that an Ecclesiastical Chart had already been published and that it was better and more comprehensive than the one she had planned. She tried to make light of her disappointment but there was very little consolation to be found. She had been so sure that at last she had discovered an outlet for her gifts, for that remarkable brain which her teachers all assured her she possessed but for which life seemed to have no particular use. She had enjoyed spending the imaginary profits of the publication, and seeing the new church at Attleborough rising at least partly through her efforts. She had even indulged in daydreams not unlike those which had been the solace of her childhood. Now there seemed to be nothing left; it had all been a castle in the air.

The chart was thrust aside in a deliberate effort to forget. She would not even admit to a sense of humiliation and frustration. Instead, she threw herself into the old routine with added fervour, to compensate for the loss of her new-found sense of purpose. Yet even this outlet, she suspected, might not be available to her much longer, for about this time she wrote to Maria Lewis: "I will only hint that there seems a probability of my being an unoccupied damsel, of my being severed from all the ties that have hitherto given my existence the semblance of a usefulness beyond that of making up the requisite quantum of animal matter in the universe." The obscure and stately prose was typical of one of Miss Rebecca's favourite pupils, but the plain fact was poignant: Isaac had fallen in love.

Perhaps it was as well that her father had already decided to take her with him on a little trip to Derbyshire and Staffordshire. He was in some doubt as to his plans for the future, and there were matters he wished to discuss with his brothers, especially with his brother William at Ellastone. The plan suited Mary Ann's restless mood. To her delight, they spent a night with Samuel and Elizabeth Evans in their tiny cottage at Wirksworth, but the visit was not wholly satisfactory. It would have taken a much younger Elizabeth Evans to penetrate Mary Ann's state of mind and heart.

Robert Evans was in the mood for sight-seeing; perhaps he as well as his daughter needed some distraction from nagging thoughts. On the way to Ellastone they passed through Ashbourne, where Mary Ann was much impressed by the beautiful parish church with its lofty spire. From Ellastone they visited the famous gardens of Alton Towers, and on their way home they spent a little while in Lichfield and saw the sights. This time, however, they dined at The George.

After their return, Mary Ann again took up her role as a devoted daughter, a capable housekeeper and a learned young lady. Everything seemed unchanged, but occasionally she unconsciously betrayed herself. She wrote long letters to her closest friends, some full of religious ardour, and some sentimental to the point of silliness. She even indulged in the Floral Language popular at the time. "I have had bestowed

55

on me the very pretty cognomen of Clematis, which in the Floral Language means Mental Beauty," she wrote to Maria Lewis. "I will send you your Floral name in my next, when I have received my Dictionary." It was a strange pastime for a girl who prided herself on her studies in French and German and Italian, but at least it seemed to bring her into closer touch with her friends.

In September she dutifully accompanied Isaac on a visit to Edgbaston, Birmingham, where his fiancée, Sarah Rawlins, lived. Mr and Mrs Rawlins were old friends of the family, so that in every way the engagement seemed ideal. Inevitably, Mary Ann's own feelings were mixed. Sarah was older than she was, older even than Isaac, and it was only to be expected that she would take her place. And although Mary Ann's special relationship with her adored brother now existed mainly in her imagination, she could not help subconsciously resenting any intrusion. It seemed inevitable that henceforth she would no longer count for much in the family circle.

Mr and Mrs Rawlins welcomed both brother and sister warmly, and for Isaac's sake Mary Ann did her best to hide her troubled feelings. Knowing that she was reputed to be fond of music, her kind hosts booked seats for the Musical Festival on two successive days. On the first occasion, they heard the *Messiah*, and on the second, selections from Haydn and Handel. Mary Ann let her puritanical scruples about listening to professional singers in sacred music go to the winds; she would forget about them for once and enjoy herself. Unfortunately, the second experience was too much for her; to everyone's intense embarrassment, she burst into tears in a sudden fit of hysteria and created a scene, the true reason for which she would have found it hard to explain, even to herself.

Fortunately the situation was soon to be resolved. Robert Evans had decided to retire from the greater part of his business and to hand everything over to Isaac, including Griff. His brothers had approved of his decision, and so had his son Robert. It was not, of course, necessary to consult the females of the family, though from as early as July Mary Ann's letters to her friends contained references to his plans. "I believe it is decided that Father and I should leave Griff and take up our residence somewhere in the neighbourhood of Coventry," she wrote in one, and in another: "My prospects have been long fluctuating so as to make it unsafe for me to mention them; *now* I believe I may say that I am not to be dislodged from my present pedestal or resign my sceptre."

Mary Ann was still to be mistress of her father's house, but they were to move to a house in the Foleshill Road, just outside Coventry. This, she realized, would be a new beginning, but it would be the end of the brother-and-sister relationship which she had struggled so hard to maintain. It would also be the end of the only secure background she had ever known. When the marriage took place, Sarah would be mistress of Griff House.

6

MARY ANN EVANS and her father moved into their new home in March, 1841. It was a big, semi-detached house, with a pleasant view of Coventry, less than a mile away across the fields. It did not take them long to settle down. They were still in the heart of their own family circle, with Isaac and Sarah, Chrissie and Edward, and Fanny (Mary Ann's stepsister) and her husband, Henry Houghton, all living within a few miles of them. Thus there were all manner of family comings and goings, including visits from Chrissie's older children, who would be sent in times of family crisis to be looked after by their young aunt, to her great delight. Mary Ann was fond of children. They also had good neighbours. Next door lived a successful young businessman, Abijah Pears, and his charming wife, Elizabeth, who had been educated at the Miss Franklins' school. She had sound evangelical views on religion and would, so the Miss Franklins decided between them, make an excellent friend for Mary Ann. The good ladies bustled round their acquaintances, trying to introduce their star pupil to suitable, sober-minded ladies and gentlemen. What about the Rev. John Sibree and his wife, Mary? They lived in Foleshill and would be sure to have much in common with such an exemplary young lady.

To bring these like-minded people together was a delightful task.

As soon as possible, Mary Ann resumed her studies. She sought out masters in Coventry and worked hard at German, French, Italian, Latin and Greek. She also took music lessons and attended lectures on chemistry. Before long her time was as fully occupied as it had been at Griff, in spite of the smaller household and the lack of farm duties. She plunged into social work, visiting the poor and the sick, and also running a clothing club with Elizabeth Pears, who was fast becoming a personal friend. She hardly had a minute to spare, but this, of course, was what she wanted. Or was it?

Everything, so it seemed, was predictable. The pious, learned, charitable Miss Evans would continue to be admired for her piety, her learning, and her good works. She would win an assured place for herself in Coventry, especially in religious circles, and everyone would respect her, even the frivolous young, who doubtless giggled secretly: "My dear, no wonder she's such a *good* young lady—with a face like that!"

Mary Ann did not need to be told that she had a face like a horse. Secretly, she was only too well aware of it. Nor did anybody nowadays need to tell her that she had an exceptional brain; she was very well aware of that too, and what was the use of it? Things would have been different if she had been a boy. Nobody, she thought, at Griff, or at school, or in Coventry, amongst her family, or her friends, or her neighbours, could imagine what it felt like to have a man's force of genius and yet to suffer the slavery of being a girl. Slavery was not too strong a word for it, yet the more she felt her chains, the more she threw herself into her household work, her studies, her music, her embroidery, her charitable activities, as if seeking a means of escape from utter frustration.

59

Nevertheless, a subtle change was taking place. She now had access to libraries and bookshops, with the result that she was reading even more widely than before, and she was also meeting people of varying types, town and country, ignorant and wise, educated and uneducated. Amongst them she was shocked to find people who professed religious beliefs but made no attempt to live by them. It was enough to profess a belief, so they seemed to think, and to live in a tolerably respectable manner. Behind the respectable façade, you could surely do as you pleased. Mary Ann's keen eyes saw through the respectable façade, and she did not like what she found there. In the back of her mind, there had long been a nagging question. The novels of Sir Walter Scott, which she had read aloud to her father, portrayed many exemplary characters who did not profess evangelical beliefs: some of them were not even Christians. If, as she believed, these novels were true to life, how could this portrayal be made to fit into the rigid pattern of her faith, especially in the light of her recent contacts with nominal, backsliding Christians?

Mary Ann did not discuss her difficulties with anybody, least of all with her father, who was settling down very happily in Coventry and gaining a feeling of importance from the position accorded to him by his fellow-parishioners at Trinity Church, where he and Mary Ann attended regularly. "I held a plate and gave a £1," he would enter from time to time in his diary. It gave him great satisfaction to be regarded as a man of substance and of sound views, and he was proud of his devout, clever daughter, so well read in theology and so active in good works. To confide in him was unthinkable. Even Maria Lewis, with whom she still corresponded very frequently, would hardly understand what on earth she was talking about if she tried to confess her vague doubts in one of her letters. She did, however, take one decision, rather abruptly. She gave up using the fanciful flower language. It was as if she had suddenly made up her mind that at least to this extent she could be honest.

Soon after she and her father had settled in Coventry, Mary Ann met an attractive young couple called Charles and Caroline Bray. She had called in next door to see her friend, Elizabeth Pears, to find established in the drawing-room a forthright, dominating, enthusiastic young man and his pretty, gentle wife. They were introduced to her as "my brother, Charles Bray, and my sister-in-law, Caroline, only we always call her Cara".

As usual when unexpectedly confronted by strangers, Mary Ann was on the defensive. She must make the right impression on these people. This was all the more important because she liked the look of them and wanted them to be her friends. She must be careful not to repel them by any trace of country speech or country manners, or to voice any opinions of which they might conceivably disapprove. Miss Rebecca herself could not have been more correct and careful.

After they had gone, Elizabeth turned to her. "How did you like Charles and Cara?" she asked.

"Very much," said Mary Ann, almost warmly though still on her guard. She was a little taken aback because they had not asked her to call.

Elizabeth was looking worried. "I love them both dearly," she said. "All the same, I would not wish you to meet them here very often. Charles is a notorious freethinker."

This seemed quite incredible to Mary Ann. Elizabeth's brother a freethinker! Had not Elizabeth told her over and over again about her pious, godfearing family, all steeped in evangelical beliefs and set in the evangelical mould? Surely

61

nobody brought up in such a family tradition could turn into a freethinker, spurning all authority in religious matters, believing just what he liked, and accepting none of the things so precious to the faith of his fathers? Charles must be little better than a heathen, and yet there had been something so very attractive about him and his wife.

"Charles is very sincere, but he will not take anything on trust," said Elizabeth. "He turned Unitarian first, and that, of course, was extremely upsetting. But of course the Hennells—dear Cara's family—are of that persuasion, and I think Cara is still a Unitarian at heart. But then Charles didn't seem to be able to believe in anything, and when Cara's brother, Charles Hennell, tried to help him, he only succeeded in upsetting his own faith and writing that shocking book, *An Inquiry Concerning the Origins of Christianity*, which made dear Charles even worse than he was before. So now you will understand why I do not care for you to see very much of him."

Mary Ann understood very well. Nevertheless, she made a mental note of the title of the book. And she still hoped against hope that the Brays would invite her to call.

Obviously Charles and Caroline Bray were not attracted by Elizabeth's plain, learned, primly-spoken visitor, with her awkward manners and her pedantic conversation. Charles thought she was just like his seven evangelical sisters, and certainly the less he saw of them, the better he was pleased. Months passed, and to Mary Ann's intense chagrin, no invitation came, nor did Elizabeth suggest taking her to see the Brays, or invite her to come in and meet them when they called. Mary Ann was disappointed. It would have been nice to make some new friends.

Then, months later, Elizabeth Pears suddenly changed her

mind. She invited Mary Ann to accompany her on a morning call at Rosehill, where her brother and sister-in-law lived. Obviously she had decided that Mary Ann was far too settled in her religious beliefs to be disturbed by Charles and Caroline's waywardness. She might even do them good. After all, she was clever, and they liked clever people.

Mary Ann wrote a letter to Maria Lewis before leaving home on that chilly morning early in November, 1841. "I am going I hope today to effect a breach in the thick wall of indifference behind which the denizens of Coventry seem inclined to entrench themselves," she wrote. She had been hurt by the seeming indifference of many of the people she had met. Trying to make friends in Coventry was like battering at a locked door. Or could it possibly be her own fault, somehow? Had she been too eager in her approaches or too dogmatic in her opinions? Or did people shun her because she was plain and awkward and unfashionably dressed? Her confidence ebbed as she returned to her letter again: "—but I fear I shall fail," she added, and then continued with heavy-handed humour: "Hope in one scale, fear in the other, alternately preponderating—such is the description of our microcosm within, to speak learnedly and sentimentally, as it behooves a young lady *what* reads."

Rosehill was a large house outside Coventry, set in a big, informal garden with smooth lawns and flowering shrubs and some fine old trees, amongst them a beautiful acacia.

"They sit out here in the summer," explained Elizabeth. "They spread a bearskin under the acacia, and sit and lie about for hours, just talking."

Mary Ann looked around her observantly, missing nothing. What sort of people were these, who lay about under an acacia tree, "just talking"? Obviously Elizabeth regarded this

63

as a waste of time. But what did they talk about? That might make a difference, she thought.

When they were ushered into the drawing room, she nearly panicked. She looked round frantically for an inconspicuous seat and chose a low ottoman by the window. Here she could watch the proceedings, listen to the conversation, and avoid being drawn into it. She did not know what she had done to repel the Brays at their first meeting, but at all costs she must avoid another fiasco. She wanted these people to like her. Charles Bray shot piercing glances in her direction, Caroline smiled encouragingly, and little by little the ice melted. Clearly the conversation at Rosehill was not "just talking"; it was about literature, about education, about philosophy, about life itself. The Brays were interested in the same things as she was; they had read the same books; they asked the same questions. Moreover, they were bubbling over with new ideas, and it did not even seem to matter very much whether or not these were sensible or practicable. Whatever else they might be, they served as good talking points. Charles was wild with enthusiasm about phrenology—"Your head, Miss Evans— pardon me!—the shape of your head is quite extraordinary!" It sounded like nonsense, of course, but it was fascinating nonsense.

At first Mary Ann joined in the conversation hesitantly, speaking slowly and carefully, and above all anxious to leave the predominant part to Elizabeth and thus avoid drawing attention to herself. Soon, however, Elizabeth was left far behind, eyeing the scene a little anxiously, because though Mary Ann was obviously making a great impression on Charles and Cara, she doubted whether it was the kind of impression for which she had been hoping.

As the two friends left the house, the Brays eagerly invited

Mary Ann to come again. "Don't wait for Elizabeth—come any time—come tomorrow," they urged her.

Mary Ann hesitated. She longed to accept the invitation, but past experience had made her nervous of presuming upon hospitality, however warmly offered.

"You *must* come!" urged Charles. "Everybody comes here especially if people think they are a little cracked!"

Elizabeth hurried her friend away. Nothing had worked out according to plan, and she felt despondent and slightly depressed. What was going to come of all this, she wondered, and well she might. You could not make friends with Charles and Cara Bray and their circle, and expect your life to continue unchanged.

Mary Ann had not the slightest desire for her life to continue unchanged. She was tired of fitting her life into somebody else's pattern and her ideas into a straitjacket of somebody else's making. Her thoughts twisted and turned in the back of her mind and everywhere she seemed trapped by her love for other people. Her father—Maria Lewis—the Miss Franklins—how could she possibly cross them or blame them for her present discontent? They had done everything for her, encouraged her, given her opportunities, opened new doors for her; she owed them far more than she could ever acknowledge. And yet—"Come any time—come tomorrow!" the Brays had said.

She was attracted back like a bee to honeysuckle, though hesitantly at first, because she could not believe that they really wanted her. Perhaps they were just being polite to Elizabeth's friend. But it was true, they really did want her, and not just for Elizabeth's sake. She knew now that there were no half-measures about the Brays. If they did not want somebody, they showed it, as they had done at that disastrous first meeting.

65

And now she knew what had been the matter. She had not been herself; she had sat primly pretending to be the kind of person her friends expected her to be. But *these* friends did not expect you to be anything but what you really were. You could say what you thought and they would accept it; you could voice your doubts and your questions and they would accept them too, and not be shocked.

Everything was now coming to a head—Mary Ann's doubts and questionings, her sense of frustration, her inward rebellion against the "slavery" of being a girl when she was conscious of a man's force of genius in her soul. She hinted in her letters to Maria Lewis that a change might be impending—"to what result my thoughts may lead I know not—possibly to one that will startle you, but my only desire is to know the truth, my only fear to cling to error." Doubtless Miss Lewis would be startled when she found that her brilliant, docile pupil was claiming the right to think for herself and judge for herself in matters of religion. What her father's reaction would be, Mary Ann hesitated to predict. The very thought of him turned her into his "little wench" again, bound closely to him because he was the only member of the family who had appreciated her as a child and tried to understand her.

On January 2nd, 1842, Robert Evans entered in his diary: "Went to Trinity Church in the forenoon. Miss Lewis went with me. Mary Ann did not go." *Mary Ann did not go.* It was unheard of; it was catastrophic; it was publicly shaming. Mary Ann did not go—not because she was unwell, not because on this particular Sunday she felt disinclined, but because she no longer believed in the doctrines and observances of the Church and refused to behave as if she did. The whole thing was incredible and utterly unreasonable. It could not possibly be tolerated. How could he, Robert Evans, "carry a plate" on

66

Sundays if his daughter openly flouted his authority and the authority of the Established Church?

Soon, as Mary Ann continued to absent herself from church, other members of the family were drawn into the quarrel. Fanny begged her to dissemble for the sake of peace; Chrissie tearfully implored her to comply; Isaac, outraged by such unconventional and preposterous behaviour, scolded her mercilessly and brushed aside her protests. He continued to berate her with harsh, cutting words. Why did she think her father was indulging in the unnecessary expense of their establishment at Foleshill? Simply to give her a good position in society and the chance to find a suitable husband. And how did she think she was going to find a husband if she persisted in such ridiculous folly?

Soon Elizabeth Pears was drawn into the controversy. She besought her friend to reconsider her decision, but in vain. Helpless in the face of such obduracy, she wished she had never taken her to Rosehill, for obviously, in her opinion, Charles and Cara were to blame.

"By no means," insisted Mary Ann. "I would have come to the same decision eventually even if we had never met."

Miss Rebecca Franklin sailed majestically into battle with reinforcements. She brought a skilled theologian, a Baptist minister, to argue with Mary Ann, but even he had to retire discomfited.

"That young lady must have had the devil at her elbow to suggest her doubts," he said, "for there is not a book that I recommended to her in support of Christian evidences that she had not read."

The Rev. John Sibree tried his hand. He and his wife loved Mary Ann dearly and they invited her to spend an evening with them, hoping that they might be able to help her and resolve her doubts. This was far harder than coping with Miss Rebecca's skilled theologian. There was an element of excitement in debating with a skilled theologian and knocking down his arguments one after another like ninepins. To differ with one's friends was quite another matter, especially if one had very few friends who really counted. The Sibrees' sixteen-year-old daughter, Mary, watched the scene intently. Secretly she loved and admired Mary Ann all the more because she insisted on standing up for what she believed to be right. As the argument wore on, the young girl saw with pitying eyes that her agitation had become too intense for her to remain seated any longer. She stood, leaning against the mantelpiece, still holding with trembling fingers the little piece of muslin on which she had been stitching during the evening.

"Now, Mrs Sibree," she said at last, "you won't care to have anything more to do with me."

"On the contrary," said Mrs Sibree warmly and in loving tones, "I shall feel more interested in you than ever."

For weeks Robert Evans refused to discuss the position with his rebellious daughter. In the end she wrote to him in desperation, trying to convince him of her sincerity and of her love for him. She was not rejecting the teachings of Jesus, but she would no longer uphold doctrines in which she had ceased to believe, or join in a form of worship which she considered to be a sham. And if this meant that it was useless to maintain the establishment at Foleshill, then she would go with him anywhere. Her only wish was to show her love for him, and to care for him, and to atone as best she could for the pain she had quite unintentionally given him.

The letter only made things worse. Robert Evans was determined to be master in his own house, and if this proved to be impossible, if he could not break his stubborn daughter's will, then he would give up the house rather than capitulate. He actually began to negotiate for its sale, and Mary Ann, despondent and despairing, decided to take lodgings in Leamington and try to earn her living by teaching. Only the lodgings all looked inexpressibly dreary, and nobody seemed anxious to employ a young lady who confessed herself to be a freethinker.

The situation was impossible and at last Isaac, thoroughly alarmed, came to the rescue. It was bad enough for him to have a sister who behaved in such an unreasonable manner, but he could not possibly contemplate the notoriety of having a father who was prepared to turn his daughter out of the house. What would become of the family reputation? Tactfully he invited Mary Ann to stay at Griff until the storm had blown over, leaving Elizabeth Pears and Miss Rebecca Franklin to work on Robert Evans.

By the end of April a compromise had been reached. Robert Evans did not really want to leave his new home, as he had threatened, and live in his little cottage at Packington; still less did he want to move to a house in Fillongley, which Mary Ann reported to be "a most lugubrious looking place". Mary Ann, for her part, did not really want to live in lodgings with strangers and seek employment where her views on life would be misunderstood and unacceptable. Moreover, neither of them really wanted to be parted from the other. One final effort made by Isaac's very understanding wife, Sarah, brought about, first an uneasy peace, and then a reconciliation. Mary Ann could return home, free to believe what she wanted and think as she liked, provided she attended church with her father on Sundays. Nothing more was to be required of her.

With an overwhelming feeling of relief, Robert Evans laboriously entered in his diary on Sunday, May 15th: "Went to Trinity Church Mary Ann went with me today." As for his daughter, sitting silently and sedately beside him, she too had felt an "inexpressible relief"; she was reconciled with her father, she had maintained her independence, and above all she was now free to abandon all but "that choice of the good for its own sake that answers my ideal".

7

"I SHUT THE WORLD out when I shut that door," said Mary Ann once to young Mary Sibree, as she closed the garden door behind her at Rosehill.

It worked both ways, of course. She was trying to live in two worlds at once. There was the world of her family, narrow, conventional, suspicious and loving, where Isaac kept a watchful eye on her, and Fanny begged her to conform; and there was the world of Rosehill, where she was free to act and think as she liked, where stimulating talk was the order of the day, and ideas—serious, thought-provoking, witty or preposterous —were the common currency. She was glad to shut out the one: she hated to leave the other.

At first she could only go to Rosehill when her father was away. Egged on by Isaac, Robert Evans resented the influence the Brays were obviously having on his daughter; he resented even more her almost complete preoccupation with them. She seemed to go nowhere else. She was still very friendly with Elizabeth Pears but, as Isaac insisted, what she needed was an opportunity to mix in respectable society. Indeed, Isaac was growing more and more alarmed. In his opinion, what Mary Ann really wanted was a husband, and the sooner she found one, the better. Otherwise she would be left on his hands when their father died, and he did not want to be saddled with an unmarried sister who persisted in behaving in an unconventional manner. After all, he and Sarah had a position to keep up, and their first duty was towards their children. He was not going to be shamed by this troublesome sister of his; she must conform in the long run, or be shaken off.

The family quarrel came to a head the following Christmas, and it ended abruptly and unexpectedly. Kind-hearted Elizabeth Pears sensed the crisis and intervened on Mary Ann's behalf. Robert Evans was very fond of her, and she tackled him with such success that he gave in completely. He did not want to uproot himself from Coventry and take Mary Ann away from the dangerous influence of the Brays; he was even willing to put up with her frequent visits to Rosehill so long as she did not enthuse to him about them when she came back; all he wanted was peace in his own home, and a dutiful daughter to look after him, and love him, and attend church with him on Sundays. It did not take pretty, gentle Mrs Pears long to talk him round and persuade him that he would lose nothing by allowing Mary Ann to visit Rosehill as often as she wished.

The ideas which were discussed at Rosehill would have surprised and shocked that earlier Robert Evans who used to drive round the Newdigate estate in his gig, with his little daughter standing between his knees. How stoutly he had upheld the government and the Church and the aristocracy, and how severely he had condemned all revolutionary ideas and every attempt at reform!

Rosehill positively swarmed with revolutionaries and reformers. As Charles Bray said, everyone who had "a queer mission or a crotchet, or was supposed to be a little cracked" was sent up to Rosehill. George Combe, the phrenologist, came every summer with his wife, Cecilia, daughter of the famous actress, Mrs Siddons. He would sit in the place of honour, in the centre of the bearskin under the acacia, and hold forth to the assembled company at such length that, so his host remarked afterwards, "it did not surprise us sometimes when his devoted wife dropped asleep in the middle of his discourse, her head inclined towards him in a reverent attitude of attention."

Some of the visitors to Rosehill were more practical in their ideas on reform. Dr John Conolly wanted to introduce humane methods in the treatment of the insane in the lunatic asylums, and James Simpson, who had known Mary Ann's hero, Sir Walter Scott, was an enthusiast in the cause of popular education. He actually wanted every child to have free elementary education, which would have seemed a preposterous idea to Robert Evans, a self-educated man who knew his place and expected everybody else to know theirs.

People of all faiths or of none were equally welcome at Rosehill, provided they had ideas and could talk. George Dawson, who liked to hold forth lying flat on the ground, was a Baptist preacher; James Martineau, brother of Harriet Martineau, was a Unitarian; and Dr Ullathorne, full of righteous indignation at the hardships, horrors and injustices involved in the transportation of convicts to Australia, was a Roman Catholic. All could be equally sure of a hearing, though not all were aware of the keen scrutiny of another frequent guest, the learned Miss Mary Ann Evans. On one occasion she wrote: "I saw Robert Owen yesterday, Mr and Mrs Bray having kindly asked me to dine with him, and I think if his system prosper, it will be *in spite* of its founder, and not because of his advocacy; but I dare say one should even begin to like him if he were known long enough to erase the first impression."

Mary Ann might have reservations about some of Rosehill's distinguished or eccentric visitors, but with the family it was another matter. She revelled in her friendship with Charles and Caroline Bray, going for long walks with Charles—to the shocked consternation of Maria Lewis—and discussing every subject under the sun with him; helping Cara with the little infant school she had started for poor children in Coventry, and playing duets with her in the evening. Cara's sister, Sara Hennell, often came on long visits to Rosehill, and here again Mary Ann found a new friend and new interests. Sara was clever, scholarly and a good linguist; she was also a lover of music, and she and Mary Ann would sing together to Cara's sensitive accompaniment. Forgotten now were all Mary Ann's theories about the dangers of secular music; she thoroughly enjoyed the musical evenings at Rosehill and took part in them with enthusiasm.

Charles Hennell, author of the *Inquiry into the Origins of Christianity* which had so shocked Elizabeth Pears, was another musical enthusiast. He came often to Rosehill, where the air seemed to suit him and the company delighted him. His health was precarious, for he was threatened with tuberculosis, and because of this he had been forbidden to marry the girl with whom he was deeply in love, Rufa Brabant of Devizes. Her father, Dr Brabant, would not hear of the marriage, but this did not stop Rufa from visiting her friends at Rosehill.

Rebecca Elizabeth Brabant had been nicknamed Rufa as a little child, on account of her red-gold hair, by the poet Coleridge, who was one of her father's patients. Rufa seemed to have everything; she was learned and well-read; she was good-looking and attractive; and she was the only child of a devoted father who was believed to be a great scholar. Perhaps this explains why at first Mary Ann Evans was less than enthusiastic about her. "I have had many pleasures since you wrote in the society of Mr Hennell and Miss Brabant," she wrote to Sara Hennell. "You wish to know that conception or misconception I may happen to have about the character of the latter. The first impression was unfavourable and unjust, for in spite of what some caustic people may say, I fall not in love with every one, but I can now satisfy your affection by telling you that I admire your friend exceedingly; there is a tender seriousness about her that is very much to my taste, and thorough amiability and re-tiredness, all which qualities make her almost worthy of Mr Hennell."

Increasingly, Mary Ann was regarded as a member of the family. Her approval was important; her opinion counted. Moreover, her companionship was sought and enjoyed. When the Brays and the Hennells went off on a five-day trip to Malvern, Warwick and Stratford-on-Avon, they wished Mary Ann to accompany them, and her father made no objection. When, in the height of the summer, they all went to Wales, Robert Evans again gave his permission for Mary Ann to have a holiday. This time Rufa Brabant joined the party, and it soon became obvious that she and Charles Hennell were determined to overcome all obstacles to their marriage. They all stayed at Tenby, and Mary Ann was so carried away by the gay mood of her companions that she forgot about all her inhibitions and frustrations and allowed herself, for once, to be young and care-free. They even managed to persuade her to come with them to a public ball, where she would doubtless have enjoyed herself as much as the rest of them if only they could have found a part-ner for her. Even the infectious light-heartedness of the Brays and the Hennells could not turn the Ugly Duckling into a Swan.

At last Dr Brabant's opposition was overcome and his consent gained: Rufa and Charles Hennell were to be married. The marriage took place at a Unitarian Church in London and Mary Ann was invited to be a bridesmaid. She spent a gay fortnight in London which made her remember with regret that dismal holiday with Isaac, when she had criticized him for his frivolity and shut herself up with Josephus's *History of the Jews*. Afterwards Dr Brabant invited her to stay for a while at Devizes and take Rufa's place until he could accustom himself to her absence. This was an opportunity not to be missed, and Mary Ann could hardly wait until her father's permission had been obtained. To stay in the home of such a great scholar and to pay him daughterly attentions would be an almost unimaginable privilege.

On her arrival, Mary Ann felt like a half-starved little cat confronted by a saucer of cream. The great scholar seemed delighted with her, and Rufa's mother, who was blind, welcomed her warmly. Her customary shyness with strangers vanished almost at once, for these people were not like strangers, and when Dr Brabant took her into his well-stocked library she expressed herself rapturously.

Dr Brabant smiled benignly. "This is *your* room, my Deutera!" he said. Afterwards he continued to call her "Deutera", from the Greek word meaning "second", explaining that he regarded her as his second daughter and that he hoped she would indeed be a daughter to him. Inevitably, Mary Ann thought of his first daughter, with her rippling red-gold hair, and a picture seemed to grow in her mind of an illustrious scholar, dependent on a devoted daughter for the fulfilment of his life's work—just such a daughter as Rufa or even, perhaps, herself. It was like one of her old daydreams.

It had never come naturally to Mary Ann to do anything by

halves. Whether she was embracing evangelical religion, or repudiating it, taking up a new line of study, throwing herself into a new friendship, it must be all or nothing. Forgetting for the time being all her home claims and duties, she followed the Doctor everywhere; she read with him, walked with him, and strained every nerve to please him. "We read and walk and talk together, and I am never weary of his company," she wrote to Cara, who had seemed a little doubtful and dismayed beforehand at the prospect of her visit. How ridiculous of dear Cara! Mary Ann was in her element, and she soon wrote to ask her father if she might prolong her visit.

She liked Mrs Brabant, though she found her a little precise and prim, and not as warmly approachable as her husband. But of course her blindness must be a terrible deprivation. To think of being quite unable to enter into her husband's scholarly activities or share in the great work on which he was engaged! She, Mary Ann, must do her best to fill the place, and so win the gratitude of both husband and wife, as well as enjoying for herself the gratification of having in some small measure helped to raise the great genius to his well-earned pinnacle of fame.

With such an atmosphere of exhilaration in the house, perhaps it was just as well that Mrs Brabant's sister, Miss Hughes, was also a member of the party. She seemed to Mary Ann to be a very practical and efficient lady, with an eye for all the domestic details which were inevitably overlooked by poor Mrs Brabant. She also showed a very proper concern for her guest.

"Now how are you planning to return to Coventry, Miss Evans?" she asked Mary Ann during the second week of her visit. "I would advise you to travel by Cheltenham and Birmingham, unless you would prefer another route."

Mary Ann thought it would be delightful to travel via Cheltenham and Birmingham. "But I have just written to my father to beg for a longer absence than I had thought of when I came," she explained. "I hope I have yet three weeks to consider about the matter."

Miss Hughes seemed to think her father would find it difficult to spare her for so long, but of course he would be all right with Chrissie and Fanny both living so near, and kind Elizabeth Pears next door, let alone their faithful servant, Mary, who was more a friend than a servant. There was no cause for worry. Her father had lots of people to look after him, whereas Dr Brabant really needed her.

When Rufa came to stay for a week after her honeymoon, Mary Ann tried to retire tactfully into the background. She must not monopolize the Doctor when his real daughter was there; on the other hand, things could not be quite the same now that she was married, with a home of her own, and he would soon need his Deutera more than ever.

Once Rufa had gone, they soon slipped back into the old relationship. "What should I do without my Deutera?" the Doctor would say, and Mary Ann would look up at him adoringly and wish she might stay with him for ever.

"I am sorry, Miss Evans," said Miss Hughes, after advising her yet again about the routes to Coventry. "My sister wishes you to leave the house as soon as possible."

Mary Ann could not believe her ears. This must be some hideous mistake. It had never entered into her head that poor blind Mrs Brabant could be jealous. There was no possible cause for jealousy. Were they not both of them devoted to serving the great genius and worshipping at his feet? Miss Hughes had completely misunderstood the situation with her nasty, suspicious mind, and Dr Brabant would soon put everything right. Mary Ann was upset, but not unduly worried. She knew he could not and would not spare his Deutera.

Miss Hughes was buzzing round the house officiously, discussing the situation with Mrs Brabant in the drawing-room, bearding the Doctor in his library—"his Deutera's room", as he had called it, but Mary Ann did not care to go there with Miss Hughes in possession. She was sending out for information about the journey—as if she had not busied herself enough about the journey!—and discussing travel arrangements in a loud voice so that everybody in the house could hear. Mary Ann could not wait for the moment when Dr Brabant would intervene.

Very slowly it dawned upon her that the moment would never come. The Doctor seemed to be quite oblivious to what was happening. He smiled vaguely; he seemed happy to let his efficient sister-in-law deal with the situation if only he could be left in peace; he shook his head at Miss Evans, as if in sorrow rather than in anger, as if she had presumed in calling herself his Deutera, and invading his library instead of respecting his privacy, and accompanying him on his walks when he much preferred to go alone. Obviously he was prepared to forgive her presumptuousness if only she would go away and leave him to devote himself to his studies as before.

Stunned and mortified, Mary Ann took refuge in her pride. She could not admit herself to have been at fault, except to the extent that she had offered her devotion to an idol with feet of clay. Retreating in good order, she returned to her father, and to her friends at Rosehill, who loved her and understood her. At the back of her mind, a lingering doubt suggested that possibly the great work of genius had existed only in her imagination. This doubt was to remain long after the hurt of the incident had gone—this, and the sure knowledge of what it felt like to be betrayed by somebody one had loved and trusted. There also remained the daydream, the unforgettable vision of the golden-haired daughter at the feet of the great scholar, only now it was indeed the golden-haired daughter, not the Deutera.

8

THE BRAYS and the Hennells were deeply concerned about Mary Ann. Cara had tried to warn her to be on her guard with Dr Brabant, but she had rushed heedlessly and enthusiastically into a situation which was bound to result in either a scandal or a humiliating retreat. In spite of her great learning and her exceptional brain, she seemed to have very little sense when it came to looking after herself. Any number of young ladies with half her intellect would have had more worldly wisdom. Nevertheless, there was about her something so lovable, so endearing, so completely lacking in self-confidence and self-esteem that they longed to help her to find her niche in life. Charles Bray, of course, was convinced that there must be a very special niche somewhere for anybody with such a remarkable head.

Some of Mary Ann's friends thought she would be happier if she were married; others were determined to find an outlet for her gifts which would bring her satisfaction. Cara innocently tried her hand at match-making, but with singularly little success. Charles, with his usual impetuosity and enthusiasm, had swept Mary Ann away with them on a visit to the Lake District, and on the way back they called on Cara's bachelor cousins, Philip and Frank Holland, who lived in

Manchester. Philip and Frank were delightful young men, and it seem to Charles and Cara such a pity that Mary Ann should be looking out of sorts.

"She was tired and unwell," wrote Cara to her mother afterwards, "and I thought looked her very worst, but you know we were only there one night and neither Frank nor Philip paid her special attention. I do wish friend Philip would fall in love with her, but there were certainly no symptoms of it."

At one time it looked as if Mary Ann's sister Fanny might be more successful. She and her husband, Henry Houghton, introduced Mary Ann to a young picture-restorer of their acquaintance; an artist, they thought, might be the very person to appeal to this shy young sister with her prodigious learning and her unconventional ideas. Her looks would tell against her, of course, but if only the young man could be given some idea of her intellectual attractions, he might be won over. In the end he was indeed won over completely; it was Mary Ann who wavered and drew back. She needed all Cara's sympathetic understanding and support to help her through this experience.

"She came to us so brimful of happiness, though she said she had not fallen in love with him yet," wrote Cara to Sara Hennell, but the happiness was short-lived, for Cara went on to explain that when he visited her at Rosehill, the unfortunate young man "did not seem to her half so interesting as before, and the next day she made up her mind that she could never love or respect him enough to marry him and that it would involve too great a sacrifice of her mind and pursuits." Gentle Cara grieved sadly for them both. "We cannot help feeling that she has been over-hasty in giving it up," she wrote. "And yet—and yet—one does not know what to advise."

The incident rankled with Mary Ann, for she could hardly bear to think of the young man's wounded feelings, of which she had been the cause. "I have now dismissed it from my mind," she wrote to Sara. "And only keep it recorded in my book of reference, article '*Precipitancy, ill effects of*'. So now dear Sara, I am once again your true Gemahlinn, which being interpreted, means that I have no loves but those you can share with me—intellectual and religious loves."

She was resolved to forget the whole affair. Nevertheless, she had learnt something from it, however painfully. Not long afterwards, she said to Mary Sibree: "How terrible it must be to find oneself tied to a being whose limitations you could see, and must know were such as to prevent your ever being understood." She could hardly bear even to imagine such a situation, but the thought of it, and the possibility of it, lingered deep in her memory.

Meanwhile the Brays and the Hennells had been more successful in pursuing the second idea for solving Mary Ann's problems. They may not have succeeded in finding a husband for her, but they did at least find a possible outlet for her gifts. Some time previously Joseph Parkes of Birmingham, a well-known Radical thinker and active politician, had suggested to Charles Hennell that the time was ripe for publishing an English translation of *Das Leben Jesu*. This was a critical and weighty study of the life of Christ by the German theologian, David Friedrich Strauss, who utterly repudiated the supernatural elements in the Gospel story and assigned many cherished Christian beliefs to the realm of mythology. The book had given rise to a storm of protests when first published in the late eighteen-thirties, and as a result Strauss had lost his position as a lecturer at Tubingen University.

Joseph Parkes considered that there were two main problems in publishing an English edition of the work: the expense involved, and the difficulty of finding a translator. He and some of his friends, he thought, might be able to provide the necessary finance if only Charles Hennell could find somebody able and willing to undertake the laborious task of translating such a long and formidable work. In his first flush of enthusiasm, Charles suggested his sister, Sara, but she very sensibly insisted that such a task would be quite beyond her powers. Eventually both brother and sister agreed that Rufa Brabant should be approached. She was a good German scholar, and she would have her father to turn to in any serious difficulty. This seemed an excellent idea until Charles and Rufa were married; afterwards, they were not so sure. Eventually they decided that somebody else would have to undertake the task, and who could be better than Mary Ann Evans? This seemed a perfect solution from every point of view, and fortunately Mary Ann accepted the proposition with enthusiasm. At last she would have an opportunity to use her learning, and especially her knowledge of languages, to some effect.

The book was fifteen hundred pages long, written in solid, scholarly German, tightly packed, with quotations in Latin, Greek and Hebrew. The work of translation took Mary Ann two years and in many ways it was a thankless task, though she gained a good deal from it, not least in establishing a literary reputation of sorts. Her name was omitted from the title page, but it was obvious that "the Translator of Strauss" was somebody to be reckoned with. On the other hand, the financial reward was hardly encouraging; for her arduous toil, attention to detail, and meticulous care in translating, she eventually received the sum of twenty pounds. If ever she had to earn her living, it seemed obvious that she would have to look elsewhere.

As the long work proceeded, Mary Ann would fall in and out of love with her task and with her author. "When I can work fast I am never weary," she wrote to Sara Hennell. "Nor do I regret either that the work has been begun, or that I have undertaken it. I am only inclined to vow that I will never translate again if I live to correct the sheets for Strauss." In one of her letters she referred to him wearily as "leathery Strauss" and complained that her brain grew "leathery" in translating him. "Glad am I that someone can enjoy Strauss," she wrote to Sara at the height of her task. " The millions certainly will not, and I have ceased to sit down to him with any relish."

Part of her trouble was that she could hardly bear Strauss's merciless dissection of the nature and life of Jesus. She herself had turned away from the miraculous element in the Gospels, she had rejected the evangelical interpretation of Christianity, she had repudiated the doctrines and dogmas of the Church, but for her Jesus was, and would always be, "the embodiment of perfect love". Mary Sibree, who in her girlhood knew her well, recorded in later life that "her reverence and affection for the character of Christ and the Apostle Paul, and her sympathy with genuine religious feeling, were very clear to me. Expressing one day her horror of a crowd, she said, 'I never would press through one, unless it were to see a second Jesus'."

The Brays and the Hennells did their best to help and encourage her, and to provide her with an occasional change of occupation or scene. Otherwise she suffered from fierce headaches, and the harder she worked, the more they persisted. Sometimes the Brays would carry her off to the theatre in Birmingham, or to spend a few days in London, and once they delighted her by arranging a tour in Scotland. Mary Ann could hardly wait to see the places which were already so familiar to her through the pages of Sir Walter Scott's novels.

Just about the time they were due to set off, a family disaster occurred, and it looked as if Mary Ann would have to give up the project, though it had originally been planned for her benefit. Chrissie's husband, Edward Clarke, who had long been in financial difficulties, was declared bankrupt, and Chrissie and the children arrived for an indefinite stay. Mary Ann was full of sympathy. She was fond of her brother-in-law, and his career had been so chequered with crises that what she did not know about the struggles of a young and impecunious doctor against adversity was hardly worth knowing. Nevertheless, it seemed hard to have to give up her own pleasure just now. She did not have very many pleasures, and the prospect of this particular excursion had meant so much to her.

Charles Bray settled the matter. Impetuous and enthusiastic as ever, he persuaded Robert Evans that Mary Ann desperately needed a holiday for the sake of her health, and no sooner had he succeeded than they set off for Liverpool and thence by sea to Glasgow and the haunts of Rob Roy.

"We were all in ecstasies, but Mary Ann's were beyond everything," wrote Cara afterwards.

It was just as well they did not know that an urgent letter from Isaac Evans was following them on their travels and missing them at every stopping-place. At Edinburgh it caught up with them at last, and conveyed the news to Mary Ann that immediately after her departure Robert Evans had fallen and broken his leg. She must, of course, return home at once.

Mary Ann was almost frantic with worry. "Please, Charles, enquire at the coach office while I pack my things," she begged.

"But we're going to Abbotsford tomorrow!" protested Sara. "You can't miss Abbotsford—not *Abbotsford*—not where Scott actually *lived*—and where he wrote the novels—you just *can't*, Mary Ann!"

"Your father would be very upset," intervened Charles

Bray. "Here, show me the letter again. Look—it says he's going on well—see?—going on well! There's no need to rush home at once, and as for travelling alone, it isn't suitable and Isaac would be horrified. You must stay one more day and then we can all travel home together."

Mary Ann allowed herself to be over-persuaded. She had revelled in the scenery and the places associated with the novels, and this final excursion was to have been the climax of it all. She looked at the letter again. Certainly Isaac described their father as "going on well", and he only said she must come home "as soon as possible", not immediately. Surely he would have said "immediately" if there had been any serious cause for anxiety. And Charles Bray was right: Isaac would be loud in his disapproval of her and of her friends if she were to travel home alone. It was not proper for a young lady to travel un-escorted.

When she actually saw many-turreted Abbotsford, with the Tweed running darkly below and the sheep moving peacefully across the sun-lit slopes, she knew this was something she could hardly have borne to miss. Here was the very place where so many of the novels had been written, the books which she had gulped down feverishly as a child, loved passionately as a young girl, and which she now read aloud to her father, thus helping in some measure to restore the old relationship between them. The world of Scott's novels had brought the real world to life for her; she had learnt tolerance from them, and an understanding of all kinds of men and women, and a respect for other people's beliefs, or lack of belief, and other people's consciences. She knew that Scott had come later than most to novel-writing; perhaps that explained why, out of the richness of a full and active life, he had so much to give.

Afterwards they lingered for a while in the golden ruins of

87

Melrose Abbey, crumbling and ivy-clad, with only grassy mounds and fallen masonry to show how great a community had once flourished there. On the western wall of the south transept, the old prayer of the master mason—"I pray to God and mari bathe & swete sanct Johne to kepe this haly kyrk fra skathe"—testified to the futility of prayer if it is to be judged by human and material standards. Whether the undying faith of the master mason and the haunting beauty of Melrose conveyed any assurance of indestructible and eternal spiritual values to the plain, awkward, frustrated young woman who wandered round the ruins on that calm, autumnal day in 1845, who could tell?

When Mary Ann returned to her father, she knew at once what her main task was to be for as long as he should live: she must fulfil the role of his loving and dutiful daughter. Henceforth her father would come first, and she would have no relaxation save for the change of occupation afforded by her arduous task of translation. She laboured on with the book, finding a stark consolation in the knowledge that she was doing the job well. She was still, as she said, "Strauss-sick", but she found help and inspiration in the little cast of Thorwaldsen's *Risen Christ* which stood on the windowsill in her study, where she could see it from her desk. She had shocked her family and friends by repudiating the Church, but she did not repudiate Jesus.

"O the bliss of having a very high attic in a romantic continental town, such as Geneva—far away from morning callers dinners and decencies; and then to pause for a year and think 'de omnibus rebus et quibusdam alliis', and then to return to life and work for poor stricken humanity and never think of self again."

Mary Ann wrote these words in a letter to John Sibree during this "dutiful daughter" period of her life. She liked and trusted young John, and sometimes she would betray herself in her letters to him in a way she seldom did with any other correspondent. Unfortunately his parents accused her of upsetting both John and Mary in their religious beliefs, with the result that the two families became estranged. To nobody else had Mary Ann confessed her longing for that "very high attic in a romantic continental town"; it may have been evoked by her feelings of envy when he set off to renew his studies in Germany, but it voiced something which went far deeper, a longing to be herself and to find her vocation in life.

For over three years Mary Ann devoted herself entirely to the care of her ageing and ailing father. Forgotten were their disagreements and difficulties, and the long drawn-out struggle over her attendance at church; once again she was the little girl who had stood between his knees as he drove about the countryside in his gig, the little girl to whom he was the fount of wisdom, the dearly-loved parent whose every word was law. She nursed him during his frequent illnesses, she took him away on holiday in search of health, she read aloud to him for hours, almost always from the works of Sir Walter Scott. The other members of the family were content that this should be so; they came when summoned, expressed their concern, their anxiety and their love, rejoiced when the patient seemed to be recovering and went away again tearfully, leaving Mary Ann in charge. She was the unmarried daughter and naturally this was her duty and her privilege.

She still enjoyed her friendship with the Brays, and when her father was in better health she would relax with them in high spirits, joining in music and fun and laughter, and helping them to entertain their guests. One very illustrious guest was Emerson, and both Mary Ann and the Brays were surprised to find the great philosopher so friendly and approachable. Emerson was deeply impressed by Mary Ann. "That young lady has a calm, serious soul," he remarked afterwards to Charles Bray, after conversing with her. She, in her turn, recognized in Emerson a genius far superior to any she had yet encountered: "I have seen Emerson, the first *man* I have ever seen," she wrote to Sara Hennell.

Some of her other friendships were gradually outgrown. Long after their intimate correspondence had ceased, Maria Lewis continued to visit Mary Ann and her father at Foleshill. in Cara Bray's opinion, she had become that "stupid Miss Lewis" who kept Mary Ann from visiting Rosehill during her stay. The Christmas of 1846 was the last occasion, however, for Mary Ann could no longer endure Maria Lewis's censoriousness. It was like having your governess continually at your elbow. When she repeatedly criticized Mary Ann for taking too much interest in people of the opposite sex, and for her free and easy behaviour, Mary Ann suddenly rebelled.

"What nonsense," she stormed. "Take an interest indeed! You might just as well say *you* have a special interest in being friendly with me!"

Maria Lewis retreated. She was hurt and upset, and decided never to visit Foleshill again. It was an unfortunate ending to a friendship from which, in the old days, stormy, passionate, intelligent little Mary Ann Evans had benefited greatly. Now she blushed to think of those long letters, full of evangelical fervour and vows of undying friendship, the early outpourings of girlish adoration and the silly, sentimental flower language. She knew Maria had kept them. Eventually she asked for them back, and Maria agreed to lend them. Once they were in her possession, Charles Bray solved the problem for her.

"You don't have to return them," he assured her. "Letters are the property of the writer, not of the recipient."

This may have seemed a doubtful proposition, but it provided a welcome solution for Mary Ann. She refused to part with a single letter but eventually, on an impulse, handed them over to Sara Hennell's safe keeping. She did not want any member of her family to discover them, and she herself had no wish to be reminded of a chapter which had definitely closed.

The translation of *Das Leben Jesu* had been an outstanding success, all copies being sold, and it seemed possible that other work of this kind might be available to her. Her publisher, John Chapman, wanted her to translate some of the writings of Spinoza, and she found the idea attractive. Meanwhile she wrote a few anonymous articles for the *Coventry Herald*, which Charles Bray had purchased, and thus gained some satisfaction from seeing her original work in print. There seemed to be no likelihood that she would be able to earn a living later on, either by translating or by free-lance journalism, yet she knew that when her father died, his estate would be shared between his five children, so that his unmarried daughter would not have adequate means of support. She had no intention of depending on Isaac. At one time, before her father's illness became acute, the Brays noted her happy, absorbed expression and suspected that she was embarking on a novel, but she soon gave up the attempt. She had too little self-confidence to persist through the early, tentative stages, and the harsh reality of her father's steady deterioration in health obtruded on the familiar world of daydreams.

During the last stages of Robert Evans' illness, Mary Ann nursed him day and night. Her whole life was concentrated on this one object, to care for her beloved father to the end, to repay with selfless devotion the love he had given to his tousle-headed "little wench" of long ago. The Brays grew increasingly worried about her. Cara wrote anxiously to Sara saying that Mary Ann looked "like a ghost". She added: "It is a great comfort that he is now quite aware of his situation, and was not in the least discomposed when Isaac told him he might die suddenly. It was quite a pleasure to see him sitting in his chair looking so calm just after he had known this; and he takes opportunities now of saying kind things to Mary Ann, contrary to his wont. Poor girl, it shows how rare they are by the gratitude with which she repeats the commonest expressions of kindness."

Cara Bray's loving partisanship and sympathy may have brought some solace to Mary Ann, but her real source of comfort lay elsewhere. She had purchased a copy of Thomas à Kempis's *De Imitations Christi*, illustrated by woodcuts, and when she turned to its contents she seemed, as she said afterwards, almost to listen rather than to read. "If thou seekest this or that, and wouldst be here or there to enjoy thy own will and pleasure, thou shalt never be quiet nor free from care: for in everything somewhat will be wanting, and in every place there will be some that will cross thee. . . . Both above and below, which way soever thou dost turn thee, everywhere thou shalt find the Cross: and everywhere of necessity thou must have patience, if thou wilt have inward peace, and enjoy an everlasting crown." This conception of "inward peace" appealed intensely to Mary Ann and it was constantly reiterated. "I have often said unto thee, and now again I say the same, Forsake thyself, resign thyself, and thou shalt enjoy much inward peace."

In those last agonizing months, as Robert Evans slowly and peacefully slipped away, Mary Ann found a strange happiness, as if for once the outward tensions of her life had eased. She sat by him in his last hours, her hand in his, and wondered how she would bear what was to come. "What shall I be without my father?" she asked desperately. "It will be as if a part of my moral nature were gone."

All her life Mary Ann had either depended on somebody she loved or been in a position where somebody she loved depended on her. Now she would have to stand alone. When Robert Evans breathed his last, on the 31st of May, 1849, it was indeed as if his little wench had died too.

9

THE EBULLIENT Charles Bray knew exactly what must be done next. Some time before Robert Evans's death, he and Cara had decided that Mary Ann would need a good holiday, so he had made all the arrangements in advance, ready to be carried out with the least possible delay when the time came. Charles enjoyed planning holidays, and this was to be one of his best efforts. They would take Mary Ann for a tour on the Continent and show her some of the sights of Europe. How her heavy face would light up! And what fun they would have, with no imperious old father to send word for her to return, and with her censorious stick of a brother at last—one might hope—unable to assert his authority over her. Charles envisaged a large party, with everyone in high spirits, but at the last minute everybody else fell away, and only Charles and Cara and Mary Ann sailed from Folkestone on the opening stage of the journey.

Mary Ann was almost completely passive. It was too soon after her father's death for her to feel anything very much. Only five days previously they had laid him to rest beside Christiana in the graveyard at Chilvers Coton Church, and she was still feeling numb from exhaustion and shock. It was no use telling her that her loss had long been anticipated; her mind refused either to accept it or to face the future. She went passively where she was taken, and even Charles's boyish enthusiasm failed to rouse her.

Charles Bray thought he had allowed ample time and opportunity for recovery. After short visits to Paris, Tonnerre and Lyons, they would travel down the Rhone by boat; nothing, he felt sure, could be more soothing and restful for poor Mary Ann. Cara did her best to support his efforts.

"How lovely!" she would exclaim. "Just look at the dear little villages nestling along the river banks—oh, *do* look, Mary Ann. Aren't they pretty? Aren't they quaint?"

"But half of those houses are in ruins," observed Mary Ann. "Just see how tumbledown and eyeless they look! The poor wretches who live in them must lead a dismal existence—I don't know how they bear it."

She brightened up at the idea of visiting Avignon. Perhaps this would be the turning-point of the holiday. However, she was too tired to enjoy it as much as she had anticipated, and in the end they travelled on to Marseilles and drove along the lovely Mediterranean coast to Genoa. It was stiflingly hot and the little seaside towns on the Riviera dazzled the eye in the pitiless glare of the sunshine. There was no refreshing green, for the countryside inland was dried up and white with dust, and even Robert Evans would have found it hard to judge the agricultural value of the land. Southward, the Mediterranean stretched to the horizon, a brilliant blue sea beneath a brilliant blue sky. Nowhere was there any refuge from the heat.

From Genoa they went to the Italian Lakes, to Maggiore and Como, and Cara enthused over the beauty of the landscape and the grandeur of the distant views. They bowled along the dusty roads to see the sights, and Mary Ann complained of headaches as she looked drearily about her, longing for the end of the day.

"Now for Switzerland!" exclaimed Charles at last. "The mountain air will soon drive away your headaches, Mary Ann, and make you feel yourself again."

This would have sounded promising had Mary Ann ever known since early childhood what it was like to feel herself.

They were to ride over the Simplon Pass into Switzerland and then go on to Chamonix. Charles and Cara were delighted at the prospect, and even Mary Ann began to rouse herself from her lassitude. Charles and Cara were hoping that at last they were about to reap some reward from their labours. After all, this tour had been arranged for Mary Ann's benefit, and so far she had shown very few signs of appreciation. All too soon their hopes were dashed. Mary Ann had been allotted a faulty side-saddle, with a tendency to slip alarmingly at critical moments. Obviously she was terrified lest this should happen at the edge of a precipice, but she stubbornly insisted on making a martyr of herself.

"No, thank you," she replied to every offer of exchange made by the other ladies in the party of travellers, ladies who were probably more experienced horsewomen and more accustomed to heights. "I prefer to keep this one."

Even gentle Cara began to feel exasperated. What could be done for Mary Ann? Was she determined to return home in the same dismal state in which she had set out?

They came at last to Geneva and stayed at little holiday resorts by the lake. A slightly more contented look began to steal across Mary Ann's heavy face. For years she had been fascinated by the idea of Geneva. When she had longed for "a very high attic in some romantic continental town", Geneva

96

had been one of the havens she had visualized. And there she was with Geneva almost within a stone's throw.

Slowly Mary Ann began to pull herself together. She knew she would have to take up an entirely different life when she returned to her own country. Her portion of her father's estate would, so she had been told, bring in about £90 a year; he had also left her £100 in cash, which with care should see her through the winter. After that, she would have to find some way of earning her living, and her mind shied away from the thought. She kept on returning to that £100 which should see her through the winter. Where? she wondered. Where? She had no home now, and she could not imagine herself spending this particular winter, the first after her father's death, in anybody else's home, especially in her present frame of mind. What she needed was to take a long, cool look at life, not to be smothered with kindness.

They were staying in Vevey, at the Hotel de Trois Couronnes, in lovely July weather. Charles and Cara were making plans for the journey home, and Mary Ann seemed to be listening passively as usual. Then, as she gazed across the still blue waters of the lake, she suddenly saw her way clearly.

"I want to stay on here in Switzerland," she said.

At first Charles and Cara were loud in their protestations. What an idea! How would Mary Ann be able to fend for herself in a strange town, amongst strangers, when she still could not face up to life in the company of her closest friends? They would not hear of such a thing! Mary Ann must return with them and share their home for as long as ever she liked. Any other arrangement was unthinkable. They quite understood that she might not wish for the time being to stay with any of her relations. Doubtless they would do nothing but criticize her whilst heaping their own burdens on to her

97

shoulders. But Charles and Cara understood her and loved her, and of course she would be happy at Rosehill.

"I know," agreed Mary Ann. "I know, dears, perfectly well. But I want to stay on here—not in Vevey, in Geneva. I've always wanted to spend some time in Geneva, and now at last I can."

She was free as she had never been while her beloved father lived, only she did not know what to do with her freedom.

Now that she had made up her mind, she seemed more composed and cheerful. Charles and Cara exchanged glances; they were sorely tempted to give in. Mary Ann had not been an easy travelling companion, and the prospect of yet another long journey in her company had been somewhat daunting.

"Perhaps—if we could find a nice, respectable pension—" began Cara hesitantly.

"The very thing!" agreed Charles, regaining some of his customary enthusiasm. "I'll take you back to Geneva, Mary Ann, and not leave you until you are comfortably settled."

Charles Bray was never one to let the grass grow under his feet. Once he and Cara were absolutely sure that Mary Ann knew her own mind and was determined to stay on in Geneva, he lost no time in helping her to carry out her plan. The town itself would be too hot for her in the height of the summer; she would be sure to suffer from the blinding headaches which afflicted her from time to time. Instead, he arranged for her to stay outside Geneva at Campagne Plongeon, on the south side of the lake, along the Route d'Hermance. The pension stood close to the lake, on gently rising ground; it was a large, comfortable house in pleasant surroundings, and there were some magnificent chestnut trees in the grounds where Mary Ann would always be able to find shelter from the scorching sun. The proprietress, Mme de Valliere, was a charming, cultured lady who ran her household efficiently and took a warm, personal interest in the welfare of her guests. Nothing could be better for Mary Ann at this troubled stage of her life, and surely nothing could be more proper—this second point would be important when the Brays arrived home without her, for they would doubtless have to justify and defend her decision to remain behind. It was not usual for unmarried ladies to stay abroad by themselves or to travel in foreign countries unaccompanied, and Isaac Evans would be sure to disapprove.

Mary Ann liked Mme de Valliere. She was essentially a kindly woman, though she was a shrewd judge of character—"I believe she has found out already that I do not know how to look after my own interests," wrote Mary Ann ruefully, shortly after her arrival. She was sure, however, that Madame would never take advantage of her ignorance; she was more likely to over-protect her and try to mother her.

All the older women at the pension seemed to want to mother Mary Ann. This young Englishwoman, so recently bereaved and so obviously homesick for her own country and for her family and friends, called forth all their motherly instincts. Her very helplessness made them want to take her in hand. How could she be content to make the very worst of her looks? Her hair was parted in the middle, drawn straight down on either side of her broad forehead, and fastened tightly above her ears; from there it hung down in incongruous ringlets, framing her long, sallow face. The style would have suited a pretty young girl, but it did nothing to help Mary Ann. She would sit glumly in the salon with her arms crossed, nursing her elbows, unfashionably dressed, and with never a word of small talk, until the kind ladies almost despaired of her. How would she ever find a husband? To be sure, she was said to be a clever young lady, but what was the use of that? If only she would dress fashionably, arrange her hair differently, stop sitting about like a broody hen and indulge in gay chatter and small talk, how much better things would be for everybody, herself included. Nobody seemed to be able to do anything about it until at last the Marquise de St Germain took command of the situation.

The Marquis and Marquise de St Germain were temporarily exiled from their home in Piedmont. They had brought with them their three children, six servants and two gentlemen said to be friends or relations, so that they were by far the biggest party at the pension and tended to dominate the scene. The Marquis was a tall man with an appalling squint; he generally played whist with his friends in the evening, but he liked occasionally to hear Mary Ann play the piano, which gratified her and helped to soothe her miserable feelings of inferiority. The Marquise came of a very old, aristocratic Italian family but at first Mary Ann was repelled by her voice and manner.

"She has a voice like a market woman!" she thought contemptuously, hugging to herself the knowledge that her own voice, even if plebeian, was low and sweet and singularly attractive.

Her attitude soon changed, however, as the Marquise became increasingly interested and friendly. It was not long before she gave in and allowed herself to be taken in hand. Relentlessly, the great lady combed out the offending ringlets, shouting her disapproval as she did so. Then, after a few tentative experiments, she arranged Mary Ann's luxuriant brown hair in two soft bands on either side of her face.

"It makes me look like the Sphinx!" objected Mary Ann.

"*Tant mieux!*" proclaimed the Marquise in ringing tones, and as all the other ladies at the pension agreed with her, Mary Ann dared not raise any further objections. She herself thought the style unbecoming. "I seem uglier than ever," she wrote to the Brays, but gradually she got used to it and made no attempt to change it.

Her closest friend at the pension was an English widow, Mrs Locke, who came from the Isle of Wight. At first she seemed inclined to be censorious, but soon Mary Ann found that she was "just the kind of person I shall like to speak to—not at all 'congenial' but with a character of her own". Mrs Locke was invariably kind and friendly towards Mary Ann, but she could be "waspish" when she felt the occasion demanded it, and two wealthy American visitors soon experienced her sting.

Mary Ann had already described the two Americans in a letter to the Brays. The mother, she wrote, was "kind, but silly—the daughter silly, but not kind, and they both chatter the most execrable French with amazing volubility and self-complacency". They were obviously anxious to impress the English visitors and lost no chance of doing so.

"I am afraid the health of our young ladies in England is not what it used to be," observed Mrs Locke one evening. "Such round cheeks the little misses had when I was young! But now I fear their health has been deteriorated by their habits."

At last the young American girl saw her opportunity.

"Surely not!" she said importantly. "*I have been to Court*, you know, and the young ladies there look very healthy indeed."

Mrs Locke drew herself up and pursed her lips.

"Oh, I belong to the gentry," she said crushingly. "I know nothing about the nobility."

She raised her eyebrows and exchanged amused glances with Mary Ann. The American girl was completely at a loss. Why were these dowdy, homely-looking English ladies so unimpressed by her presentation at Court? Back home, everybody would be all agog to hear the whole story down to the smallest detail. What she had heard was all too true; the English were a stiff-necked lot who looked down their haughty noses at free-born American citizens.

Mary Ann described the scene in a letter to the Brays, and others followed thick and fast. The little group at the pension came alive in her descriptions. Other visitors came and went, and soon the Brays were familiar with every one of them: Mademoiselle Ross, "rather a nice creature but with a mere woman's head and mind"; poor homesick Mademoiselle Elise, the *gouvernante*; Madame Cornelius, "daughter of the richest banker in Frankfort and, what is better, full of heart and mind with a face that tells you so before she opens her lips"; Monsieur de Herder who "would be a nice person if he had another soul added to the one he has by nature—the soul that comes by sorrow and love"; two young German brothers, "the eldest odious, with an eternal simper and a mouth of dubious cleanliness. He speaks French very little, and has a miserable splutter between a grunt and a snuffle so that when he begins to speak to one one's brain begins to twist and one feels inclined to rush out of the room. His brother frowns instead of simpering and is therefore more endurable." On further reflection she added: "After all they are very harmless young men and I fancy very rich—'so the world will love its own'." There were also sweet little Mademoiselle de Phaisan, "extremely prosy, and full of tiny details; but really people of that calibre are a comfort to one occasionally, when one has not strength enough for more stimulating things. She is a sample of those happy souls who ask for nothing but the work of the hour, however trivial—who are contented to live without knowing whether they effect anything, but who do really effect much good . . .";

and Mrs Wood, who sympathized with Mary Ann about the tea—"The tea of the house here is execrable—or rather, as Mrs Wood says, 'How glad we should be it has no taste at all—it might have been a very bad one.' I like the Woods—they are very good-natured. Mrs Wood a very ugly but ladylike little woman who is under an infatuation as it regards her caps, always wearing the brightest rose-colour or intensest blue, with a complexion not unlike a dirty primrose glove. Mr Wood is an old gentleman, a thorough man of the world who makes one feel quite *cosy* when he sits by one with his little jokes and fireside way of talking about everything."

The little world of the pension was etched clearly in her letters to the Brays, though only occasionally in the letters she wrote to her brothers and sisters. The Brays, she knew, would understand, whereas everything she described would be so alien to her home-keeping, conventional family that for the most part it would be quite outside their comprehension and therefore, probably, slightly shocking. She did write to them, however, frequently and at length, always begging for a reply, especially when Chrissie's nine-year-old Clara died and her heart was torn with sorrow for them all. For the most part, their replies were few; Fanny was her best and also her most understanding correspondent.

Unfortunately she could not resist pouring out everything in her letters, especially when writing to the Brays. She was homesick, of course, but naturally she would not admit it. She wanted to receive more letters; she was worried because her boxes of books had not arrived; she was preoccupied with her own health—"I am better but not well"—"My limbs ache terribly sometimes"—"I have never been well since I came." When she retired to bed with a headache, all the ladies at the pension invaded her room with kind enquiries and an incessant chattering which only made her worse. Even a pleasure trip had its drawbacks. She joined a party in M. de Herder's boat for the Fête de Navigation and they rowed out on to the lake at sunset. "When the moon and stars came out there were beautiful fireworks sent up from the boats. The mingling of the silver with the golden rays on the rippled lake, the bright colours of the boats, the cannon, the music, the splendid fireworks, and the pale moon looking at it all with a sort of grave surprise, made up a scene of perfect enchantment." Only she could not resist adding that she had "rowed all the time", and describing all the aches and pains she was enduring—"I have almost lost the use of my arms with rowing."

Above all, she was lonely. When things happened which hurt her—and she was all too easily hurt—there was nobody at hand to cushion the blow. In spite of Mary Ann's determination to stand on her own feet, there was something in her nature which was so exquisitely sensitive that she could not bring herself to

> *"welcome each rebuff*
> *That turns earth's smoothness rough,*
> *Each sting that bids nor sit nor stand but go!"*

The stings simply paralysed her and made it impossible for her to move. Quite small things upset her. She was delighted to receive a letter from Mary Sibree and then found that she was asked to direct her reply to Rosehill, because Mary thought her father might object to the correspondence. Mary Ann's pride was deeply wounded. "Please to give my love to her," she wrote to the Brays, "and tell her that I cannot carry on a correspondence with anyone who will not avow it." When John Sibree called, she was convinced that he had come out of curiosity—"*impertinent* curiosity," she insisted. Worst of all,

Sara Hennell repeated some remarks made by her husband which made Mary Ann collapse into bed with a headache.

"I am quite timid about writing to you," she wrote to Charles and Cara when she recovered, "because Sara tells me that Mr Hennell says 'there is much that is morbid in your character (his observations were upon your letters only) with a dwelling on yourself and a loving to think yourself unhappy.' Nothing can be truer than the observation, but I am distressed and surprized that this is so very evident from the letters in which I have really tried to avoid everything which could give you pain and have imagined that I have only told you of agreeables except the last, which I hope you understood to be playful in its grumblings. I am ashamed to fill sheets about myself, but I imagined that this was what you wished."

Eventually, restless and unsettled, she decided she no longer wanted to stay in the pension, where people came and went, and where nobody seemed to have any roots. Also she dreaded the winter at Campagne Plongeon, for everybody told her that it would be bitterly cold, and they would probably be snowed up for weeks. She thought of spending the winter in Paris, which would be nearer home, but she decided that the expense would be too great. Besides, all the ladies in the pension assured her that it would not be proper for her to stay in Paris alone; at her age, she must not think of such a thing. "I thought my old appearance would have been a sufficient sanction and that the very idea of impropriety was ridiculous," she wrote in a letter to the Brays, but she bowed to the general opinion. "As long as people carry a Mademoiselle before their name, there is far less liberty for them on the Continent than in England," she observed.

In the end, she began to contemplate the idea of spending the winter in Geneva, but in private lodgings in the town.

She was not ready to go home yet. In any case, she had no home to go to. Somehow she would have to begin to come to terms with life, and nobody else could do this for her. She paused at the end of a long letter to the Brays and then, on a sudden impulse, added: "Good-bye, dear creatures. Keep me for seven years longer and you will find out the use of me, like all other pieces of trumpery."

Why seven years? Mary Ann, carefully folding and sealing her letter, had not the slightest idea. Nor, understandably enough, had the Brays.

"O THE BLISS of having a very high attic in a romantic
continental town, such as Geneva!" Mary Ann had
written in one of her long letters to John Sibree. A
very high attic—not a respectable pension in a select neighbourhood at some distance from the town. She was restless and
dissatisfied, and she went on making excuses to everyone concerned, herself included. Campagne Plongeon would be too cold
in winter; she would have more facilities for study in Geneva
itself; she was tired of the constant succession of guests—
"people so little worth talking to"—and her friend, Mrs Locke,
had already left, with a last warning at parting: "You won't
find any kindred spirits at Plongeon, my dear!"

When at last she found her high attic, it looked so unprepossessing that she almost lost heart. After more than one
disappointment, she had been advised to visit a Monsieur and
Madame D'Albert Durade, who were said to be looking for a
paying guest. They sounded as if they might possibly be congenial; the husband was an artist, and both he and his wife
were musical, cultured people, with an interesting circle of
friends. Everything sounded very promising, until she saw the
house.

It was a typical stark, blank-faced house with shuttered

windows, rising high above the cobbles of the Rue des Chanoines. The grim darkness of the entrance was relieved only by a glint of autumnal sunshine from the courtyard beyond. She stood, uncertain where to go next, and as she waited she shivered involuntarily, though it was a warm and pleasant day. The very air felt damp and chill. At last she realized that the staircase was immediately on her right; she could hardly see it through the gloom. Slowly, hesitantly, she began to climb the winding stone stairs.

At the first landing, she paused. She would not go a step further. It was impossible, unthinkable. She could not contemplate living in such a dreadful, cheerless place. The forbidding staircase continued to wind upwards, with narrow windows at intervals through which one caught glimpses of the world outside. Perhaps she ought to explore a little further. No step in life had ever been particularly easy for her. Even finding a high attic might involve more effort than she would willingly have given. She trailed on up the dark stairs with very little hope of discovering anything worth while at her journey's end.

The landing was singularly unattractive. She stood outside the door of the D'Albert Durades' apartments while she recovered her breath. She even hesitated before she rang the bell, but at last she pulled herself together and rang it with such resolution that she could hear it tinkling madly in the distance. A pretty young housemaid opened the door. She stood looking up into Mary Ann's face with a trusting, childlike smile, before, remembering her training, she bobbed a curtsey and invited her in.

As Mary Ann entered the comfortable salon, its occupants rose to greet her. She suppressed a start on seeing M. D'Albert Durade for the first time. She had been told that he was deformed, but she had not realized the extent of his deformity.

He was a dwarf, barely four feet high, with a twisted spine, but his head was of normal size, tilted slightly upward. He had iron grey hair, slightly curling, and thin, expressive features, and his eyes, which were keenly penetrating, beamed friendliness and kindness.

Madame came forward with a welcoming smile. Mary Ann took to her at once, for she looked motherly and capable and as if she genuinely cared about people and what happened to them. Her home would surely be a haven—a high attic, in fact, both literally and metaphorically. There were two sons, pleasant, well-mannered boys, who waited courteously in the background and then came forward to be introduced. The elder was Alphonse, the younger, Charles. As Charles bowed, Mary Ann noted his handsome looks and poetic expression. His father might have been just such an attractive fellow had it not been for his deformity.

Her misgivings were fast disappearing. Why worry about the dreary stone stairs when they led to such an attractive, homely place? She was offered a large room, with an alcove in which the bed was placed, so that it looked more like a sitting-room in the daytime.

"Would you object if I hired a piano?" she asked.

"But of course not—we love music!" said Mme D'Albert Durade. "You must play on this instrument too, whenever you wish. And you will join our musical evenings, I hope, and meet our friends, so that we can enjoy making music together."

It seemed too good to be true. Perhaps the rent would be beyond her means. She asked a little anxiously and was promptly reassured.

"One hundred and fifty francs a week," Mme D'Albert Durade told her.

"And how much extra for light?" asked Mary Ann.

"But of course that *includes* light," said Mme D'Albert Durade. "And your meals, which you will take with us, except for *le petit déjeuner*—you will prefer to take that in your own room, doubtless?"

Mary Ann could hardly believe her good fortune. Apart from a momentary pang on tearing herself away from the chestnut trees at Plongeon, glowing in their autumn colours, and from the view of the lake close at hand, she felt no regrets on leaving the pension. She could hardly wait to be installed snugly in her high attic with the hospitable D'Albert Durades.

The life at 107 Rue des Chanoines suited Mary Ann. She soon became attached to the house which had seemed so grim and uninviting, and it was not long before she felt thoroughly at home there. Her comfortable bed-sitting room had been arranged by Mme D'Albert Durade in such a way as to make her feel like a member of the family rather than a paying guest. Even the pictures had been carefully chosen; obviously there had been no question of decorating the room with rejected oddments. The one she liked best at first sight depicted a handful of brightly-coloured flowers scattered across the pages of an open bible.

"What a lovely painting!" she had exclaimed on her first visit. "The colours are exquisite."

"I am happy to know you like it so much, Mademoiselle," Mme D'Albert Durade had observed with a smile. "It is one of my own."

So Madame was more than an admirable housewife and mother—she was an artist. Not so good an artist as her husband, perhaps, but an artist nevertheless. How fortunate Mary Ann was to have found a home for herself in such a household! And how easy it was to establish a happy relationship with the family! They were interested in the same things; they enjoyed similar pleasures; and there were no secret jealousies and mis-understandings to mar their growing friendship such as had wrecked her visit to the Brabants. She could not imagine M. D'Albert Durade behaving like Dr Brabant, or Madame scheming resentfully like Mrs Brabant and Miss Hughes. She was quick to tumble into the same irrepressible enthusiasm and affection—"For M. D'Albert I love him already as if he were father and brother both," she wrote to the Brays, and Charles Bray raised his eyebrows with a quizzical smile, wondering what was to come next. But Madame understood the situation perfectly. This plain, awkward, inhibited young woman needed security; in short, she needed loving and understanding.

"Call me Maman!" said Mme D'Albert Durade, and she proceeded to mother Mary Ann, and also to spoil her a little because she looked as if nobody had ever managed to break down her inhibitions sufficiently to spoil her. The Brays were the exception, but by the end of the holiday their patience had been wearing a little thin. Madame's patience knew no limits; her husband's deformity and her understanding of it had created between them that tenderness from which spring compassion, and upholding love, and the patience in which, as Christ said, men and women possess their souls.

Naturally Madame soon began to drop the formal "Miss Evans" and "Mademoiselle" in favour of "Marianne" or even occasionally, "Minie". Mary Ann welcomed the change. She liked the name "Marianne", and ever since her schooldays in Coventry she had used it occasionally when signing her letters, instead of the more formal "Mary Ann". In Geneva she was always "Marianne", and she might have been tempted to use it permanently had there not been a suspicion of something frenchified about it which might not find favour at home.

Besides, the pronunciation would be a difficulty; "Marianne" was attractive in French, but at home people sometimes pronounced it "Mary-anna", which was nearly as bad as "Mary Ann". The Brays and the Hennells often called her "Polly"; in letters to them she occasionally signed her name as "Polly", or sometimes "Pollian"—a clumsy variant of Apollyon which embodied a private joke between herself and Sara. It would be nice to use a name which everybody liked and took for granted. Gradually she decided to become "Marian Evans" when she returned home. To use a new name might possibly symbolize the changes which her high attic had brought into her life.

She had always known that she would love Geneva. She liked the narrow cobbled streets, some of them steep and winding, the painted houses, the red roofs, the unexpected little squares and courtyards, and the grey cathedral with its twin towers. "Maman" would encourage her to take walks, especially when she was plagued by one of her frequent headaches, and she would wander round the old town, still with its fortifications, though rumour said these were soon to be pulled down, and still with its reminders of human aspirations and religious controversy. When she returned to 107 Rue des Chanoines, there would be a touch of colour in her sallow cheeks and a heightened animation in her manner. She soon found that a five minutes walk would take her right out of the town and into the open country, where she could see the peasants working in the fields and the country people taking their wares to market. If she wanted to venture further afield, M. D'Albert Durade would accompany her, adding to her pleasure by his friendly, intelligent conversation, and discussing with her every subject under the sun. They even went up the Petit Salève one day in a spell of the lovely autumnal weather typical of Geneva before the winter sets in, and Marian revelled in the views of the snow-clad Jura and the glittering wonder of Mont Blanc.

The winter was quite another matter. She had known it would be grim, but it was worse even than she had expected, with almost continuous mountain mist, and bitter cold, and a piled-up weight of snow. Day after day she sat by her window in her high attic, peering into the mist, and watching the little Sisters of Charity go in and out of the house opposite on their errands of mercy. They always looked happy and serene, as if they had a purpose in life and a strength to sustain them. Even as she revolted against their religion, Marian envied them for what it had given them.

At times Marian was almost tempted to give up the attempt to work out her destiny. The Sisters of Charity did not seem to look beyond the needs of others and the ever-recurring calls for their help and sympathy and compassion. Perhaps you could be perfectly contented doing the kind of work which naturally comes to a woman's hand, thus crowding out the other side of you, the intellectual powers which were lying dormant and which nobody seemed to want. Charles Bray wrote to ask if she was still interested in the idea of translating Spinoza, and she repelled the suggestion in no uncertain manner. Behind her apparent security and comfort in her high attic, she was unhappy—"in a state of discord and rebellion towards my own lot", as she confessed years later in a letter to M. D'Albert Durade. With the kind of obstinacy and perversity which spring from intense frustration, she turned away from the ambition which had brought her little else save disappointment. In a letter to Charles and Cara she wrote: "the only ardent love I have for my future life is to have given me some woman's duty, some possibility of devoting myself where I may see a daily result of pure calm blessedness in the life of another."

This was all very well, but where and who was "another"? Her family did not want her; where, save in marriage, was that "woman's duty" likely to appear? And what chance had she of marriage?

Restlessly, she tried to crowd out her discontent. She attended lectures on physics, she studied mathematics; she read voraciously; she practised her music and attended the musical evenings arranged by the D'Albert Durades with enthusiasm and keen enjoyment. M. D'Albert Durade, watching her closely, thought he knew something of the reason for her discontent. After all, he had had to learn to live with his own disability.

"I would like to paint your portrait," he said suddenly one day. "If you would permit it, and if it would not be too boring for you."

At first Marian was almost indignant.

"But why?" she demanded. "What an extraordinary idea!"

M. D'Albert Durade smiled and shook his head. He knew perfectly well what he was doing. He wanted Marian to come to terms with her looks as he himself had come to terms with his deformity. Until she did this, she would have no inward peace of mind.

"The true seeing is within," he said. "That explains the imperfection of portraiture, for the most part. We paint what we see superficially and it is good, but insufficient; we try to paint what we see with the inward eye, and only the great masters can convey it."

Marian shrugged her shoulders. "The idea of making a study of my visage seems to me extremely droll," she said. "Still, you are welcome to try."

"I shall try," M. D'Albert Durade assured her. "But I shall not succeed."

He did not succeed, of course. He knew very well that he had not succeeded. The face which looked out of the canvas was a simpering mask—"*une poupée*" as he described it afterwards. There was no hint of the turbulence, the rebellion, the frustrations and yet, behind the idealized features, there lurked the suggestion of latent powers. He liked it well enough to paint a copy for her to take home, and she liked it well enough to accept the copy gratefully.

She would have to go home eventually, of course. You could not live in a high attic for ever. Nevertheless, there was a sense in which you could take the high attic with you, as a kind of inward sanctuary. "Give me my scallop shell of quiet"—that was what she had enjoyed in her high attic, and there was supposedly no reason why she should not enjoy it at home, if only she had a home to enjoy it in. Judging by the warmth of the assurances of welcome she had received from her family circle and from the Brays, she was likely to be spoilt for choice.

Once she had decided that she was ready to go back to England, she could hardly wait to be gone. It was only as the time for the journey drew near that she realized how she was dreading it. The weather was bad, and there was no possibility of crossing the Jura by diligence. The hazardous journey would have to be made by sledge, and her imagination boggled at the thought. Charles Bray would have made light of the adventure, she knew. She began to realize at last how cushioned she had been when she had travelled with the Brays. If only M. D'Albert Durade could accompany her, how simple everything would be. But she could not possibly afford to pay his fare in addition to her own, so this was not to be thought of. Eventually the kindly D'Albert Durades sensed her anxiety, and it was decided that he should indeed travel with her, but at their expense. Thus the last barrier was removed, and Marian Evans was all set for the journey home.

It was not easy to bid goodbye to Maman and hear her saying *"Au revoir, Minie! Au revoir, chérie!"* with a final tender kiss on parting. It was even more difficult to thank her, because what Marian had to thank her for could not be put into words. It had been more than a high attic, and more than a much-needed mothering; it had been an experience of that security in human relationships which can create a growing point for life.

II

IN HER high attic, looking out over the cobbled streets and the red roofs of old Geneva, revelling in the warm, friendly atmosphere of 107 Rue des Chanoines, it had seemed clear to Marian that the obvious place to enjoy security in human relationships was in her own family circle. Distance had indeed lent "enchantment to the view". As she had read their letters, assuring her of a loving welcome in their homes if only she would return, her heart had been full of happy memories. Isaac was again the adored brother, partner in every adventure and every lively escapade, and only barred from her daydreams because he was a big boy and had put away childish things. Chrissie was again the gentle, pretty, sweet-natured elder sister, and Robert and Fanny the grown-ups who could be relied upon to protect the "little wench". She would go back to them all and begin again. She knew she would have to go out and earn her living, but at least she would have the security of their love.

Afterwards she wondered why she never seemed to be able to learn from experience. "My return to England is anything but joyous to me," she wrote to Patty Jackson from Griff, "for old associations are rather painful than otherwise to me."

No place could be more charged for her with the emotion

evoked by old associations than Griff. There was the attic window from which she and Isaac had watched the stage coach go by—the stage coach itself long since vanished and mouldering away in some old barn with the chickens roosting where the driver used to sit flourishing his whip, and mice nesting in the upholstery. The white fantails still fluttered in the yard, their feathers gleaming in the sunlight; the garden was bright with flowers and the fruit bushes held out promise of a future harvest to be raided in due course, doubtless, by her nephews and nieces. The green fields, the copses, the still waters of the canal were all there, apparently unchanged. Nevertheless, everything had changed.

"It was some envious demon that drove me across the Jura to come and see people who don't want me," wrote Marian to Sara Hennell from the haven of her dreams, which now seemed to her nothing but a dismal country with dismal people —made worse by dismal weather.

Naturally Isaac thought he was conferring a great benefit on his younger sister by inviting her to visit Griff and enjoy his hospitality. She seemed to ignore the undoubted fact that she was the failure of the family, the one sister who had not succeeded in finding herself a husband. It appeared extraordinary to him that she could not settle down for a while and devote herself to womanly tasks. It would not do for her to stay too long, of course, but there could be no doubt that he was amply fulfilling his duty as her brother and her nearest male relation.

Marian was convinced that Meriden would be different. Dear, gentle Chrissie would welcome her and make her feel at home, and she would be able to help her a little, and share her anxiety over the health of her husband, and her grief for the death of her darling Clara, and her constant, niggling worry over the state of the family finances. Actually things did not work out like that at all. Chrissie's welcome was wholeheartedly loving and sincere, but she had very little time to spare, and the children ran riot in the overcrowded house and made intimate conversation almost impossible.

It was all too clear that Marian had lost her high attic. She spent some months at Rosehill, but even Rosehill could not supply what was lacking. The Brays were as kind and loving as ever; there were the same comings and goings of family and visitors, the same absorbing conversation under the old acacia tree, the same music-making, the same sparkle of light-heartedness only dimmed by the increasing illness of Charles Hennell, now fatally stricken by tuberculosis. It was clear that the romance of Charles and Rufa, which had made those long-ago days at Tenby so radiantly happy, was drawing to its close.

Marian was still part of the family circle at Rosehill, yet she was becoming increasingly aware that she must break away from them all, as she had broken away from her own family, if she wanted to work out her destiny. And still she had no idea what the nature of that destiny might be, or whither it would take her. To her family, she was a failure; to her friends she was an object for compassion—gifted, lovable, but still an object for compassion; to herself, she was an enigma, an enigma which she seemed powerless to solve.

One of the visitors who came to Rosehill that summer was Bessie Parkes, daughter of Joseph Parkes who had financed the publication of Marian's translation of *Das Leben Jesu*. The girl came all the way from Birmingham on purpose to see the wonderful, learned Miss Evans; secretly she cherished literary aspirations, and here was a chance to meet a real, live author. It was a pity Marian was suffering from one of her blinding headaches. She was kind; she tried to smile; but she could not respond to the glowing hero-worship in the girl's eyes. Nevertheless, she remembered her. She did not have so many admirers that she could afford to forget even one of them.

Another visitor was John Chapman, who had published *Das Leben Jesu*. He brought with him William Mackay, author of another of his publications, a book entitled *The Progress of the Intellect, as Exemplified in the Religious Development of the Greeks and Hebrews*. They wanted Marian to write an article on it for the *Westminster Review*, and she pounced on the idea eagerly. Perhaps this would lead on to further opportunities of the kind. She liked writing articles; she had already proved her worth as a translator; surely she could look to earning some kind of living with her pen.

In late November, when the dank countryside round Coventry was settling into winter and London, in spite of rain and fog, was beginning to be gay, Marian took the finished article to John Chapman's office at 142 Strand. John and Susanna Chapman lived on the premises with their young children Beatrice and Ernest, and the governess, Elisabeth Tilley. The house was a large one, and as the publishing business was not very prosperous, the Chapmans augmented their income by taking in paying guests. Susanna Chapman was not a very good manager, but the establishment was popular, especially amongst literary folk and overseas visitors. Writers, philosophers, critics and would-be authors came and went at 142 Strand, and the ordinary run of paying guests could be sure that, though the meals would seldom be served on time, they would meet interesting people and hear good conversation at this rather unusual boarding house.

John Chapman's Friday evening literary parties were famous, and to Marian's great delight she was there for one of them. Naturally she was carried away with excitement. At first she held back shyly, but she was soon encouraged by the attention she received. After all, she had a right to be there. She was the translator of Strauss.

A young lady with sharp eyes and spectacles advanced towards her, and Marian was irresistibly reminded of young Martin Chuzzlewit and the "literary ladies" or "L.L's" in America.

"May I introduce Miss Eliza Lynn Linton?" said John Chapman, and Marian started with pleasure, for this was a real "L.L.", not a bogus one.

"Oh, Miss Evans, how delightful it is to meet you!" gushed Miss Eliza Lynn Linton. "Such a crowded party—so many tedious people—let us have a little chat."

Marian was almost mesmerized by the spectacles, and the flattery, and the aura of celebrity surrounding this undoubtedly literary lady. And how astonishing it was to find that the famous Miss Eliza actually liked her!

"I was never so attracted to a woman before as to you, my dear," she assured her, patting her hand as she agitated her fan. "You are obviously such a lovable person!"

It never occurred to Marian to look behind the spectacles and catch the malicious gleam in the shrewd, mocking eyes. She drank in every word with eagerness; she must be sure to remember to tell Charles and Cara about all this when she wrote to them. They seemed to think she would not know how to take care of herself in London, whereas already she was accepted in a literary circle and admired by literary people. If Miss Eliza Lynn Linton could earn a living with her pen, why should not she herself fare even better? She could tell at once that Miss Eliza had not a tithe of her intellectual powers and massive learning; obviously *she* could never have fulfilled the rôle of the translator of Strauss. A hint of superiority crept into her voice as she strove to impress her new friend, and the "literary lady" noted it as she withdrew. She also noted the provincial appearance, and a certain lack of breeding, together with an "unwashed, unbrushed, unkempt look" which added a spice of malice to a tale which would undoubtedly grow in the telling.

Marian was delighted with her fortnight in London and could hardly wait to return. Any doubts expressed by the Brays were indignantly brushed aside. The Chapmans' home was going to be her "high attic", with the added attraction of a succession of interesting fellow-guests. John Chapman would be another M. D'Albert Durade, except that he was young and handsome and dynamic instead of deformed and gentle and retiring. She could not imagine Susanna Chapman inviting her to call her "Maman", but she seemed harmless enough and doubtless they would soon be good friends. She had not paid much attention to the governess, except to notice that she was young and pretty, and something of a favourite with John Chapman.

As usual, Marian was rushing into a situation before she fully comprehended it. The prospect of living in London and earning her living as a writer was far too exciting to admit of any hesitation or reservations. She had known, almost from the first encounter, that she had far more qualifications to be regarded as a "literary lady" than had Miss Eliza Lynn Linton. The Chapmans' home was the centre for an acknowledged literary circle. She had won the entrée by sheer merit, and she must now strike quickly, while the iron was hot. John Chapman was a publisher; he was also on the look-out for a literary journal which he might control; he knew the right people and could introduce her to them, so that above all she must gain and keep his favour. Obviously she must go to London and settle in at 142 Strand as soon as possible. The one thing which might have made her pause was a curious letter from the governess, Miss Tilley, which was quickly followed by another in the same vein. Obviously Elisabeth Tilley was an unbalanced young woman with an obsessive devotion to her employer and a neurotic jealousy of any female, attractive or otherwise, who ventured into his orbit. She would have to be on her guard, but as for altering her plans—that would be unthinkable. She packed her bags and left Rosehill with a light heart and high expectations. Only she did at least restrain her excitement sufficiently for John Chapman to notice that her manner was "friendly, but formal and studied", when he met her at Euston.

It was impossible to maintain a "formal and studied" manner with John Chapman for very long. He was so attractive, so magnetic, and apparently so appreciative of intellectual power in a woman that Marian found it impossible to resist his charm. Soon she threw caution to the winds, only to find herself faced by what seemed to her to be a quite inexplicable hostility on the part of the ladies of the house. Nothing she did was right, apparently. She hired a piano for her room, with the assistance of Mr Chapman, who kindly helped her to choose it. She was pleased when he came to her room to hear her play and expressed warm appreciation of her rendering of Mozart, but she was extremely puzzled by the pointed way in which Susanna Chapman insisted on the immediate purchase of a piano for the drawing-room—"then we can *all* enjoy Miss Evans' music," she said. It was, of course, delightful to find that John Chapman was interested in the study of German, and wanted her to give him lessons in the quiet of her room, but it was rather upsetting to be confronted with Elisabeth Tilley's querulous indignation because nobody had offered to teach *her* German, though everybody knew she had always wanted to learn. It seemed as if John Chapman could not even suggest a walk in her company without either Susanna or Elisabeth clamouring for exercise. How different this was from Geneva, where she and M. D'Albert Durade could walk together for as long as they wished, discussing almost every subject under the sun, and then return to the "high attic" and be sure of Maman's loving welcome.

It seemed that John Chapman did not mind how many adoring females graced his home. He only objected to their quarrels, which disturbed his peace of mind. The situation was perfectly satisfactory from his point of view. He was convinced that Marian's intellectual gifts would be very useful to him some time, and he did not want to lose sight of her. At the moment, however, it was difficult to explain the exact capacity in which he was likely to need her, and it was very embarrassing to have Susanna and Elisabeth fluttering round them like a couple of angry, pecking hens, and accusing them of holding hands.

For a while, Marian stood her ground. She was not going to be driven away by an atmosphere of petty jealousy. After all, she had as much right to live there as any other paying guest. Only, at the back of her mind, there was a lurking feeling that she understood John Chapman better than Susanna did, and far better than Elisabeth; that if only he had met her first, life might have been very different.

Nevertheless, she was driven away at last, back to Rosehill, with no literary distinction to her credit and with her career no further advanced than it had been when she set off so hopefully for London. True, she had been asked to prepare an analytical catalogue of John Chapman's publications, and the importance of the task might have been regarded as conveying some kind of recognition of her gifts, but even this aroused such bitter protests from Susanna that for the time being she gave up the undertaking in resentment and chagrin.

How provoking it was that after she had gone, with no apparent prospect of return, John Chapman should at last have achieved his wish, the control of a literary journal! It was gall and wormwood for Marian, but it was also frustrating in the extreme for John Chapman. Through the generosity of an eccentric, he was to take over the *Westminster Review* in the New Year, and he was eagerly anticipating the credit, the power and the distinction which this position would win for him. Unfortunately, he knew perfectly well, in his heart of hearts, that he had neither the ability nor the education to qualify him for the job. He needed a partner: somebody who would do the work of editor without recognition, or even adequate remuneration. He only knew one person who could be relied on to fulfil such a rôle, and that was Marian Evans, exiled to Coventry.

Letters sped to and fro, domestic battles raged, until at last John Chapman broke free and visited Rosehill. In vain he insisted at home that this visit was to Charles Bray, who had indeed invited him most warmly. Elisabeth was so furious that she hardly spoke to him for three days. There was no mistaking her attitude, or Susanna's; they were determined to prevent Marian Evans from returning to 142 Strand.

In the end they were powerless to prevent it, but nevertheless, they soon found that their fears were no longer necessary. John Chapman's enthusiasm for the *Westminster Review* swept away all Marian's doubts. He enlisted her help; he set her to work on the prospectus for the periodical under its new management; but he also shattered her latest daydream.

One day they were resting on the grass at Kenilworth Castle in the warm May sunshine. Marian was well content. He needed her, and somehow or other they would solve their problems, in spite of Susanna and Elisabeth and their petty jealousies. They despised her because of her appearance, and because in many ways she was unlike themselves, but they could never give him the intelligent companionship he so sorely needed.

"I love this place," he said. "I was a little disappointed at first, but I find it grows on me."

Marian was too happy to talk much. She listened to him holding forth on his pet, long-winded theories about the "elements, characteristics and beauties of nature", and how these were wonderfully and mysteriously embodied in men and women, in a perfect balance with one another. The scene was unforgettable—the mellow ruins of the castle, the close-clipped turf, the trees still in the freshness of their spring green, the blue sky above, the singing of the birds and the haunting fragrance of the flowers.

"Ah—beauty—beauty!" he mused. "What a mysterious quality it is, and what a spell it casts upon us! A man could sell his very soul for beauty and count the world well lost—and has done—ever since Helen and the burning of Troy."

For beauty? For beauty? Must it always be beauty? Was there no other attraction for men, had there never been any other attraction for men, beyond that of a pretty face? Must men always live and die and be driven mad for Helen's sake?

> "Was this the face that launched a thousand ships
> And burnt the topless towers of Ilium?
> Sweet Helen, make me immortal with a kiss!"

Was beauty the only thing that mattered then? And was everything else a sham and an illusion?

Suddenly Marian burst into tears and John Chapman ceased

soliloquizing. He could see that her enjoyment was at an end, but he could not see the shattered daydream. Only he suspected that somehow or other he had hurt her feelings and he was sorry. Perhaps she was weeping because she was conscious of her own lack of beauty but surely, he thought, she must have got used to that by this time.

12

ARIAN EVANS returned to 142 Strand on September
29th, 1851. She had proved herself indispensable to
John Chapman for the preliminary work on the *Westminster Review* and he was tired of going all the way to
Coventry for consultations with her. The first number under
his management must be ready for January, and nobody else
could be relied upon to see the job through and take no credit
for it. If Susanna and Elisabeth still objected, he would just
have to put up with it; they could not make more fuss than
they had done already over his visits to Coventry.

Once John Chapman had made up his mind, he would
brook no further delay. As for Marian, she had found her feet
again at Rosehill. She always did. But it was never easy for her
to find her feet alone; whether the trouble came from her
family, or from her friends, or from the awkward situations
into which she was apt to rush so blindly, she invariably needed
help in extricating herself. Rosehill could always be relied upon
to give that help, but would Rosehill always be available? The
Brays had troubles of their own, she knew, for Charles Bray
had suffered business losses and the future was uncertain. Rosehill was indeed her second home, and the Brays her second
family, and what they had given her would always be part of

her life, but she surely could not for ever run to them for sanctuary. If only she could learn to be independent, she might even find out what kind of person she really was, and what her exceptional but apparently useless gifts were intended for, and what, in fact, life was all about. Nobody else could do this for one, it seemed, and yet she desperately wanted somebody.

Marian settled down quietly into the life of the household at 142 Strand, and the watchful Susanna and Elisabeth found no particular cause for jealousy. She worked hard and tended to resent the constant interruptions—"I get nothing done here, there are so many *distractions*," she said, when writing to Rose-hill. Nevertheless, she rather liked the endless comings and goings of interesting people, the guests from near and far, the famous and the not-so famous who crowded the literary parties, the authors who came to discuss the prospects of the *Westminster Review* or to talk over their proposed contributions. They, in their turn, began to respect this quiet, competent young woman who showed such an extraordinary grasp of intellectual matters on the one hand and of practical details affecting the production of a literary periodical on the other. They all noticed her attractive voice—low in volume, beautiful in tone, with the slight restraint natural to anybody who has shed a strong local dialect. Country people, for the most part, think in dialect for years after they assume what is generally regarded as correct speech, which is why the familiar tongue of childhood often returns to them in old age or *in extremis*.

This was the year of the Great Exhibition, and people were flocking to London to see its marvels. Marian visited it more than once and enjoyed it. She was there on the final day in October when it closed, and thousands of people were swept away in a patriotic fervour as their voices joined in the mass singing of *God Save the Queen*. It was "*un beau moment*", said Marian afterwards, even though she paid for it with one of her worst headaches. Thomas Carlyle, calling at 142 Strand, expressed himself very differently. He had no patience, so he said, with the Prince Consort and his advisers and their ideas, but his main objection seemed to be to the hordes of visitors who had thronged London for as long as the Exhibition remained open. "You can't get along Piccadilly for them," he said indignantly. "And I've been worn to death with bores all summer, invading my study and saying 'Here we are!'"

It was fascinating to meet the well-known writers of the day in such an informal manner. Marian had more sense now than to rush at people. She held back at first and proffered her opinions only when encouraged to do so. Soon she was liked and respected, and her advice was valued and sought after. Miss Evans, with the quiet voice and the kind eyes, was somebody to be reckoned with in the literary world.

She still found it difficult to make friends. When Fredrika Bremer, the Swedish authoress, stayed with the Chapmans, Marian was completely put off at first. "She is old," she complained in a letter to the Brays, though the famous writer had only recently celebrated her fiftieth birthday. Old? She was worse than old, for she seemed to Marian positively repulsive and utterly unprepossessing. "I have to reflect every time I look at her that she really is Fredrika Bremer," she wrote a little later, cured once and for all of literary lion-hunting. Yet before long she repented of her hasty judgment, for they proved to have many things in common. Fredrika sketched and painted and played the piano; Marian loved art and was no mean musician. Soon the days were passing all too quickly, and both were sorry when Fredrika's visit came to an end.

About this time Marian met another writer whose looks, like Fredrika's, were a handicap. She was visiting Jeffs' bookshop in the Burlington Arcade with John Chapman when they were confronted by a little man whom Marian considered to be almost aggressively ugly—"a miniature Mirabeau!" she said afterwards.

When John Chapman introduced him as George Henry Lewes, Marian recognized the name at once, for he was to be amongst the first contributors to the new *Westminster*. She knew that he had a brilliant brain and a ready wit, and a reputation for being good company, but she was repelled by his manner and appearance. He was short, slight and quick-moving, and his face was deeply pitted with the traces of small-pox. He gesticulated all the time, like a foreigner, and even during such a brief encounter he talked incessantly. She decided that she did not like him very much.

Marian now tended not to like people at first sight, perhaps because she had learnt to mistrust her own immediate reactions. Even when Harriet Martineau called at 142 Strand she held back in doubt, though the stout, energetic lady certainly seemed to be doing her best to be friendly. It may have been partly because Harriet was an established writer with a considerable degree of fame. There was something subconsciously galling about these meetings with celebrated female authors. Marian was not jealous, or even envious, but as she met them one after another, Eliza Lynn Linton, Fredrika Bremer, Harriet Martineau, she could not feel that their talents were so outstanding as to be infinitely superior to her own. Yet she was still unrecognized.

Some of the visitors to 142 Strand invited her to their homes and, once she had overcome her initial shyness, she enjoyed these contacts with a wider world. She often dined at the home of Joseph Parkes, who had financed the translation of *Das Leben Jesu*, and who had a great respect for the translator. His daughter, Bessie Parkes, still adored the great Miss Evans; she loved to watch her descending the great staircase on the arm of her host with quiet dignity and grace, always wearing a gown of black velvet, which was unusual in those days for unmarried ladies. Marian, normally so devoid of dress sense, knew exactly what to wear on such occasions. She also knew exactly what not to wear, for she would refuse invitations to fashionable balls for lack of a ball gown.

It was not long before Bessie Parkes sought to renew the acquaintanceship started on the day when she had come to Rosehill as an impressionable schoolgirl to see the wonderful, learned Miss Evans. She was still impressionable and still inclined to hero-worship, which made Marian hold back a little, though she admitted that Bessie was a "dear, loyal, ardent creature". Bessie, however, was not to be repulsed, however gently. She wanted to sit at the feet of the great scholar, but she also wanted encouragement for her own literary ambitions. Like many another talented girl, Bessie fancied herself as a poet, and again like many another talented girl, she longed for the reassurance and approval of somebody whose opinion she respected. Marian dealt with her very understandingly. Obviously nothing would stop the girl from having her poems published, since her father had considerable influence with John Chapman and could provide the necessary means. She did, however, urge her to "work on and on and do better things still", and with true insight into youth's problems, she placed herself on the same level as her disciple: "I too will try to follow my own advice," she promised.

The friendship between Marian and Bessie gradually came to mean a great deal to them both. Hitherto Marian's chief women friends had been Cara Bray and Sara Hennell, both loyal and devoted, but slightly older than herself and enjoying a security which she had so far lacked. She looked to them for advice and support, whereas here the positions were reversed. Bessie, though secure in her parents' love and her comfortable, cultured home, yet yearned to try her wings in the wider world to which Marian, she felt sure, held the key.

With Bessie came one day her friend, Barbara Leigh Smith. This time there was to be no holding back. "Your noble-looking Barbara," Marian called her, and from that first impression the adjective "noble-looking" remained somewhere in the back of Marian's mind as an ideal of womanhood. Barbara, with her rippling red-gold hair, clear eyes and sensitive features, her utter scorn of fashion and convention, her love of art and her passionate belief in the rights and potentialities of her own sex, was a character to be reckoned with. Hers was a friendship to be sought.

For the first time, Marian was offered friendship on equal terms. Barbara's brain may not have been of her own outstanding calibre, but she had so many things which Marian lacked: beauty and poise and self-assurance; a gift for painting and a knowledge of arts and crafts; encouragement at home and the freedom to express her own opinions. She also had financial security. Her father believed in treating his daughters in exactly the same way as he treated his sons. Barbara had been given a good education and trained to think for herself and form her own judgments; at twenty-one she had been given a generous allowance and encouraged to spend it as she wished, even to the building of a country cottage in Sussex, where she could entertain her friends and live her own life. What a contrast to Marian's own upbringing and her constant difficulties with censorious relations!

Marian was still smartingly conscious that she was the family failure. She was plain, she was unattractive, she had not found a husband, she made silly mistakes which landed her in embarrassing situations, her employment was unremunerative and Chapman's affairs were constantly in such a muddled state that nobody could count on the permanence either of his publishing house or of the *Westminster Review*. What had she to show for her years of study and her hard work, or even for the hidden daydreams which never even came to life? Nothing, it seemed to her sometimes, except a crop of headaches and frustrations.

For a while it seemed as if the situation might yet be changed. Soon after her return to the Strand, Marian formed a close friendship with the philosopher, Herbert Spencer, whose book, *Social Studies*, had been published by Chapman. Like Marian, Spencer came from the Midlands and, again like Marian, he was a scholar and a music-lover. He reviewed drama and opera for *The Economist*, and as their friendship grew, he would often take Marian with him to the theatre or the opera house. He also liked to walk with her on the terrace of Somerset House, where they could pace to and fro, undisturbed, watching the traffic on the river and discussing the many interests they had in common. Sometimes they would go to Kew Gardens, where Marian would tease him about his botanical theories—"If the flowers don't fit in with them," she would say, "*tant pis pour les fleurs!*"

Marian had never before enjoyed a friendship with a man who shared to such a superlative degree her academic interests and cultural pursuits and he, on his side, found in her an intensely interesting companion, his equal, he felt, in discussion and argument, so that his brain was stimulated by her company. He had been in the habit of spending an occasional evening with the Chapmans, for he lived close by, on the opposite side of the road, and now his visits rapidly became more frequent. Always he sought out Marian, and always her companionship enriched his thinking, so that he would sit until late in the evening, formulating his theories and propounding his ideas, to the all-too-obvious delight of any of Marian's friends who happened to be present. Everybody seized on the idea that they were absolutely made for one another. It would be a perfect match of like with like. As soon as the Brays realized what was going on, they plunged in with enthusiasm and urged them both to come to Rosehill together as soon as possible.

For a while Marian's daydreams ran away with her. Here at last was a great scholar to whom she could devote her life; here was an opportunity for her to fulfil that "woman's duty" of which she had written and achieve the desired result: "pure, calm blessedness in the life of another". Then gradually it dawned on her that Spencer was holding back. When he kissed her, it was a very platonic kind of kiss. When they walked together in the country, it was just such a comradeship as she enjoyed with Barbara. On the rare occasion when he voiced his appreciation he assured her that she was the most admirable woman, *mentally*, that he had ever met. Subconsciously, she accepted the situation. Yet again her appearance was too great a handicap for love—yet was it love? Suddenly she realized that if she interpreted it as love, she would lose a friendship which meant a great deal to her.

At last Herbert Spencer and Marian Evans put their cards down on the table and were honest with one another.

"We have agreed that we are not in love with each other and that there is no reason why we should not have as much of each other's company as we like," wrote Marian to the Brays. "He is a good, delightful creature and I always feel better for being with him."

Marian had made up her mind. She would take what life offered. She would not ask for more.

13

H ERBERT SPENCER's friendship with George Henry Lewes often seemed a little surprising to people who did not know either of them very well. Herbert Spencer, in spite of the occasional twinkle in his eye, seemed so learned, so preoccupied with serious things, whereas to all outward appearances George Henry Lewes was such a little clown of a man, "bonny wi' ugliness" as the Scottish saying goes, full of jokes and funny stories which were not always suitable for a mixed company. No wonder Mrs Carlyle called him "the Ape". And yet she and others of his friends seemed to know another side of him, a side which he did not care to disclose to anybody and everybody. There was, so Mrs Carlyle declared, "no spleen or malice or *bad* thing in him."

In spite of her initial dislike, Marian found him amusing. Shortly after their first meeting in Jeffs' bookshop, she met him by chance at the theatre, where she was attending a rather poor performance of *The Merry Wives of Windsor* with Herbert Spencer and John Chapman. He shared a box with them, and most of their uncontrollable laughter was caused by his running commentary and not by the antics on the stage.

"This is a farce in five acts," he said at one point, when the play seemed as if it would drag on for ever. "If it were in one act, and one didn't see it, it would be very well."

From time to time Lewes called at 142 Strand and rattled away cheerfully, to the utter disruption of Marian's work. It was all very well for John Chapman and Herbert Spencer to put up with this nonsense; they seemed to have all the time in the world, whereas she was driven by this terrible sense of urgency, this need to make a success of something, even if it was only somebody else's literary venture. She needed money too, though actually very little was forthcoming as a result of her efforts.

Marian did not very much mind being short of money for her own needs. In any case, she was used to it. The little income left in trust for her by her father was not enough to live on, and her earnings were disappointingly small. Now, however, she had other claims. Just before the Christmas of 1852 Chrissie's husband died suddenly, leaving her with six children to bring up and no more than a hundred pounds a year to live on.

As soon as she received the news of her brother-in-law's death, Marian hastened to the rescue, but there seemed to be little she could do. Isaac was in control, doing everything that was right and proper, and she hesitated to interfere. It would be much more sensible, she thought, to return to London and try to step up her earnings in order to help Chrissie financially. Unfortunately she did not ask Isaac for advice, and when he found that she had decided to leave without first consulting him, he flew into a passion.

"Very well, you must go your own way," he stormed. "But don't ever come to *me* for help, that's all!"

Marian bit back an angry retort. She wanted to say that she had never asked him for any help and that she had not the slightest intention of doing so, but she held her peace for

Chrissie's sake. She was sure he would be good to Chrissie—
"though not in a very large way," she said afterwards to the
Brays.

After her return to London she worked doubly hard, but
always with a nagging anxiety at the back of her mind. Chrissie
wrote to her about all her problems. Should she let her eldest
boy accept an offer of sponsorship in Australia? What was she
to do about an offer to find places for her younger children in
an "Infant Orphan Asylum"? How could she bear it if they
were taken away from her? In the end the little family managed to stay together, and Marian continued to help them as
best she could.

In the circumstances, it was rather strange to find her objection to Lewes weakening. She was pleased rather than otherwise when he called, even if he upset her routine. She was
beginning to catch glimpses of an acutely sensitive nature behind all his lively nonsense, as if he sensed when people were
in difficulties and in a very subtle way reached out to them
with unspoken and completely unembarrassing sympathy. Perhaps she had misjudged him and perhaps, worse still, she had
allowed others to misjudge him. She began to slip little comments into her letters to the Brays, explaining that Lewes was
better than he had seemed to be at first sight. He was indeed "a
man of heart and conscience, wearing a mask of flippancy".

"A man of heart and conscience," wrote Marian, and yet she
knew that London gossip was scandalously busy with his name.
His marriage had originally been a very happy one. He and his
lovely young wife, Agnes, had been "as merry as two birds",
according to their good friend, Thomas Carlyle, working together, making music together, enjoying the company of their
friends and, above all, of their enchanting little sons. Then,
rather suddenly, everything changed. Mrs Carlyle who had

139

always thought of them as "a perfect pair of love-birds" noticed that "the female love-bird appears to have hopped off to some distance and to be now taking a somewhat critical view of her little shaggy mate". Agnes had deserted Lewes for his friend, Thornton Hunt, and the marriage was completely broken up. It all sounded sufficiently sordid, so Marian thought, and yet she could not associate anything sordid with Lewes. She wondered even more what lay behind the mask of flippancy, and her very wonder conveyed a measure of sympathy.

Throughout that summer their friendship grew and deepened. Marian received an invitation to spend a holiday in Switzerland and in all probability she could not have explained even to herself why she had refused it. Instead, she spent six weeks at St Leonards, visited occasionally by Lewes. When she returned to London, she began to look for new lodgings. She wanted to be independent of the Chapmans, free to come and go as she would and to entertain such visitors as she wished, unscrutinized and uncriticized. Charles Bray began to complain that her letters were uninteresting and she did not try to refute the accusation. The main interest of her life at present could not be shared even with her closest friends.

Gradually the mask had been withdrawn and Lewes had laid bare the utter misery of his life. He had loved his wife and she had betrayed him for his friend; he loved his sons, and could not make a home for them; he saw no solution to his problems and no hope for the future. All he could see at the moment was that at last he had found somebody who cared enough to understand his dilemma and to feel some compassion for him. There could be no question of divorce under the existing laws. He had condoned his wife's behaviour at first and forgiven her infidelity, and this apparently involved him in some share of the blame. Moreover, even if he were to make an attempt to free himself and her, the crushing expense would be quite beyond his means. He was trapped, and he knew it, and there could be no release for him within the law.

It did Lewes good to talk about his troubles and Marian was a ready listener, all the more so because he did not want her, or anybody else, himself included, to apportion the blame. All he wanted desperately was for somebody to listen and to understand. This intense need was a new experience for Marian. All her life so far she had been the problem child, the difficult daughter, the failure of the family; she had gone to other people with her troubles, to Maria Lewis, to the Brays, to the D'Albert Durades, and this had seemed the natural order of events. Now a different order prevailed, and somebody else's despair was tugging at her heartstrings.

Marian's new home was in Cambridge Street, Hyde Park Square, a quiet backwater in the angle of Edgware Road and Bayswater Road, close to Hyde Park where she could walk to her heart's content, often with Lewes at her side. Here he could come to her with his anxieties and difficulties as often as he wished, and here she could in some measure smooth them away. Overworked herself, with her editorial duties, and her articles to write, and a book to translate from the German for which she was to be most miserably paid, she still found time to help him with his writing and even, when she was nearly driven mad with blinding headaches, to take it over and do it for him.

It was a state of things which could not last, not for a woman of Marian's integrity. George Henry Lewes was the man of her choice, but he would never be free to marry her, not for as long as Agnes lived. It was certain that the law would give him no redress. Must his life be made a misery for ever? Or should they continue to lead a kind of double existence, hiding the truth from their friends as if they were ashamed of it? Marian had no doubts. She would accept neither course, for herself or for him. It was his duty to support the wife who had deserted him and the children he so dearly loved, and this he must continue to do, with her most willing help. But his duty being fulfilled, he was free, if not in the eyes of the law of the land, then morally, in the sight of God and man. By that higher law she considered herself bound to him, for better, for worse, for richer, for poorer, in sickness and in health, to love and to cherish, till death should part them.

Once the decision had been made, Marian Evans and George Henry Lewes considered themselves to be most truly and indissolubly married. Marian paid a last visit to Rosehill in June, but she said nothing of their plans. She had consulted Charles Bray in strict confidence, but she could not bring herself to tell Cara and Sara. Dear as they were to her, they might misunderstand, for they disliked George and mistrusted him, and they would almost certainly disturb the peace of this last visit by trying to dissuade her. It would be better to leave things as they were, to spread the bearskin under the acacia and recall old times. It would be something for all of them to remember in days to come.

On the 20th of July, 1854, Marian and George left London together and sailed for Antwerp. The night before, Marian had scribbled a note to Charles and Cara and Sara.

"Dear Friends—all three,
I have only time to say goodbye and God bless you. Poste Restante Weimar for the next six weeks and afterwards Berlin.
Ever your loving and grateful
Marian."

She did not write to her family, nor did she tell them anything about the position for over two years. Then at last she wrote a loving letter to Isaac informing him that she was now married, and signing herself Marian Lewes. He replied through his solicitor with a request to know when and where the marriage had taken place. Failing to find any satisfaction in her reply, he broke off all relations with her and, on his insistence, Fanny and Chrissie did the same. No other course seemed open to them. The family failure had become the family disgrace.

14

"YOU OUGHT to try your hand at writing a novel, Polly!"

How often had George said this to her and she had laughed him off? It was only when he expressed doubts on the subject that her determination at least to try was strengthened. He thought she might lack dramatic power, whereas how could she tell until she had tried and failed? Only she hated to fail in anything, and so she held back.

For years she had wondered about the possibility of writing a novel. She had never thrown away the opening chapter she had written during the early stages of her father's illness, when she had suddenly begun to look so happy that the Brays were sure she must be writing a novel. It had all come to nothing, but the manuscript was still there amongst her papers. At one time, when they were in Berlin, she showed it to George and then suddenly snatched it back again.

"Come on, read it to me, Polly," he said.

It would not do, of course. She had known all along that it would not do. But there must have been something about it which appealed to him, for as the months went by he kept on reminding her: "When are you going to begin, Polly?"

George had faith in her. She had never had much faith in herself, because in spite of her gifts, and her mental qualities, and her capacity for hard work, she had not been able to find her niche in a world which was not interested in her because she was plain.

So far all the urging and all the determination were on his side. She was beginning to be tempted, but she kept on deferring it. She had enough work to do already, work which was contracted for, and for which in due course she would be paid. It was foolish to indulge in daydreams.

They were spending a few weeks at Tenby when matters came to a head. She was dozing in bed one morning, idly wondering if she would ever get to the point of writing a story, and what on earth it would be about if she did, when suddenly she was shocked wide awake. She had been dreaming about writing a story and she even remembered its title: The Sad Fortunes of the Reverend Amos Barton.

When she told George, he burst out laughing. "Oh, what a capital title!" he exclaimed. "Go on—write it!"

It was the first story of her first work of fiction, *Scenes of Clerical Life*, and by the time she had finished the third and last story in the book, she was famous. "A writer who can work out his simple theme thus quietly and efficiently needs no further commendation or exhibition on our part," said *The Times* critic. The stories were published first in *Blackwood's Magazine* and then, by Blackwood's, in book form. It was exactly seven years since she had written that curious letter from Campagne Plongeon, asking the Brays to bear with her for another seven years. She would not use her own name. At first she would not use any name at all, until she realized that some kind of pseudonym was necessary. She chose the name George Eliot—George because it was the name of the man she loved best in the world, and Eliot because it was "a good, mouth-filling, easily pronounced word".

It was a long time before anybody discovered who George Eliot really was, and Marian was prepared to lie about it rather than be found out. She feared lest other people besides Isaac should consider her a "disgrace" and so shun her books. Indeed it was only when an impostor, a Mr Liggins, laid claim to the authorship that she gave up the pretence and acknowledged her work. By that time her novels had far too strong a hold upon the public for the avowal to make any difference.

For some of her readers, the identification of the author was no great matter; they pounced upon her books as the instalments came out, and loved them for their own sake. For some, it was a nine days wonder, an opportunity to revive a scandal and embellish it with rumours, and from such George protected Marian by interposing an impenetrable barrier. He knew that Marian had an infinite capacity for being hurt, and he considered it part of his lifework to shield her, so that she might be free to fulfil what he believed to be her destiny.

A few of the readers whose opinion Marian valued most were at first full of misgivings and then completely won over in the deepest sense. The veteran diarist, Crabb Robinson, wrote of *Adam Bede*: "I would rather so excellent a book was written by any man than a woman, and worse, that of all women the translatress of Strauss should be the writer." Next day he added: "I do not like to state to any one that so admirable a book has been written by a woman whose history is at least so unfortunate as Miss Evans'." It was some time before he capitulated, but he never wavered in his admiration for her work. Mrs Gaskell, whom to know was to love, went further. "Oh, do say Miss Evans did not write it!" she wrote to her publisher, and again, "Will you please contradict, if you can,

the statement that Miss Evans is the author of *Adam Bede*."
She felt so strongly about it that she was positively eager to believe in the impostor, Mr Liggins, and to support his bogus
claims. When she realized the truth, however, she wrote a letter
to Marian telling her how "earnestly, fully and humbly" she
admired her work. "I never read anything so complete and
beautiful in fiction in my whole life before."

In Maggie Tulliver, the heroine of *The Mill on the Floss*,
Marian created a character very like herself and gave her a
character very like her own. But she could not resist making the
uncouth, unkempt, misunderstood little girl grow up into a
beauty. Somehow, somewhere, the ugly duckling must turn
into a swan. The truth of the matter was that the ugly duckling
which was Mary Ann Evans, the difficult child, the family
failure and the family disgrace, did indeed turn into a swan,
but she might beat her wings for ever against the barriers of
prejudice and harsh convention in her native Warwickshire
without convincing her family of the fact. Fanny and Chrissie
relented eventually, but Isaac was not reconciled until, at the
end of her life, heart-broken at George's death, she married
their friend John Cross and so became, in her brother's opinion,
an honest woman.

Safe in the high attic created for her by George's love and
constancy, Marian at last fulfilled her destiny. One knew now
what kind of person she really was, and what her exceptional
but hitherto apparently useless gifts were for, and what life was
all about. And so, like all great artists, she was free to create
what a later writer, Lascelles Abercrombie, has called a "significant world", and to say the things about life which she was
born to say.

All the significance of her past experiences came to life in her
books. The stories in *Scenes of Clerical Life* may be uneven, but

they are alive. They convey the realities sensed by the little child who drove about the countryside in her father's gig, standing safely between his knees; by the schoolgirl who felt the strong pull of evangelicalism and took sides passionately in small-town religious controversy; by the young woman who realized that the familiar world in which she had grown up was passing away.

Adam Bede brought that same world to life with such a sure touch that it lives on imperishably with its virtues and its weaknesses and the essential values which were part of a country life which has gone. Into the life of farm and dairy, of hall and workshop and village church which Mary Ann Evans knew so well, was woven the story which had made such an impression on her in her girlhood, the story told by her Aunt Elizabeth of the young girl she had accompanied to the scaffold with the assurance of God's redeeming love. Only when she idealized remembered characters or tried to bend her own creation to her will did Marian's sure touch falter. Her Adam, modelled on her father, never really comes to life; her pretty, wilful, enchanting Hetty is alive to her finger-tips. But above all and beyond all, Ellastone and the surrounding countryside and its people live on for ever. The little girl who could not explain to Chrissie and Isaac what it felt like to see Ellastone with the church tower riding high, or to look down into the clear waters of the Dove from the old stone bridge at Norbury, had grown up to create a significant world.

The Mill on the Floss may purport to be set in Lincolnshire, but every detail of the early part of the story cries out for recognition as belonging to that vanished Warwickshire where Isaac and little Mary Ann "roamed the daisied fields together". Here, in Tom and Maggie Tulliver, is the brother-and-sister relationship which never lost its radiance for Marian in retrospect. Because of that radiance we accept it all of a piece, and see Tom through Maggie's eyes in spite of our mistrust of him. The idealized Tom is true because he is true to Maggie's conception of him, but the development of Tom into a thoroughly unpleasant, selfish young man is also true, because the seeds of this development are there from the beginning. Marian could accept Isaac, but she could not bring herself to accept Tom, and so brother and sister are swept away by the river which flows through the whole of the story, the river which represents the tide of life over which they have no control. And though the forced ending seems as remote as the tombstone, with its inscription "In their death they were not divided", from the brother and sister who were so deeply separated in life, the book itself is too strong for its spell to be broken. Thus the significant world of Isaac and Mary Ann's childhood lives on long after Isaac's betrayal; the aunts who dominated their youth are still vital long after their sway is over; and all the imaginary world of Dorlcote Mill pulses with the remembered spell of Griff.

Silas Marner was the last of the books to recreate in this particular way the countryside of Marian's childhood, the rural world which even as she absorbed it was slowly passing. She herself said the theme was suggested to her by a "recollection of having once, in early childhood, seen a linen weaver with a bag on his back", and there is an element in it of Wordsworth's definition of poetry which "takes its origin from emotion recollected in tranquillity". Though it is more richly peopled and more eventful, it has something in common with Mrs Gaskell's *Cousin Phillis* in that one accepts it without question.

To accept *Romola* without question, one must read it when young, devouring it in great gulps like Scott and never trying to look behind the scenes. Marian herself said that she began

Romola a young woman, and finished it an old one. All her learning, all her historical knowledge, all her exact care for typographical detail were poured into this story of fifteenth-century Florence, and yet she could not give it life. The pageantry is there, but not the heart. It seemed as if in trying to copy life, Marian failed to create life. Romola herself is an idealized picture of Barbara. "She has that way of walking like a procession," said Monna Brigida in the story. The real Barbara may have walked like a procession, but the simile ended there. Barbara's "procession" took her out into the world where, the battle now over, she is still honoured as "Madame Bodichon", the fearless pioneer of Women's Rights and one of the founders of Girton. Romola's procession belongs to an old Italian painting; it winds on remotely and for ever, and never steps out of the frame.

Felix Holt opens with a journey by stage coach through the same long-vanished countryside as before, with the patient cart-horses waiting at the blacksmith's door and the basket-maker peeling his willow wands in the sunshine. The story, however, concerns the great house and its secrets, and the town with its thronging life, its respectable church and its sober dissenting chapel, its busy market, its populous inns, its confident rich and its submerged poor, and its occasional outbreaks of violence as seen by the young girl who had stayed with Maria Lewis when the Election Riots were raging through the narrow streets of old Nuneaton.

In *Middlemarch*, above all else, Marian said what she had to say about life. There, within the compass of a little Midland town, her characters work out their destiny and at last their author does not once attempt to bend them to her liking. Once created, they are free. And though some of them may echo in their lives the experiences of their creator, though it may be said, for instance, that Marian could hardly have created Mr Casaubon had she not known Dr Brabant, characters and situations alike are transmuted into a significant world which has its own life and never degenerates into a cardboard copy or counterfeit. People have to abide by their mistakes, as they do in real life, and the test is whether they face up to them or let them fester. Dorothea Brooke makes her mistakes, and abides by them, and suffers for them. We are tempted to prefer her sister, Celia, because Celia seems to be somebody we can know and understand, whereas Dorothea soars beyond our comprehension and sometimes beyond our patience. Yet at the close of the book we know what it is all about. "Her full nature, like that river of which Cyrus broke the strength, spent itself in channels which had no great name on the earth. But the effect of her being on those around her was incalculably diffusive: for the growing good of the world is partly dependent on unhistoric acts; and that things are not so ill with you and me as they might have been, is half owing to the number who lived faithfully a hidden life, and rest in unvisited tombs."

In *Daniel Deronda* nobody gets his heart's desire—not Daniel and Mirah, because they so seldom come to life, and only the living have a heart to feel desire, and not Gwendolen because, alive, passionate, and utterly convincing, she brings about her own nemesis. This was Marian's last novel, and to some it seems far removed from the earlier pastoral ones, which have so much of her own experience woven into them. Yet here is a great deal that went into the making of George Eliot from the young Mary Ann, the night fears and terrors, the blind rushing at fate, and above all the frustrated, rebellious protest: "You may try, but you can never imagine what it is to have a man's force of genius in you and yet to suffer the slavery of being a girl."

151

Marian Evans became a great novelist when she found the "high attic" which symbolized that inward peace which at last enabled her to create a significant world. The rest of her story belongs to history. Perhaps the message of her life may be found at the close of the book which is regarded as her one, magnificent failure. "We can only have the highest happiness, such as goes along with being a great man, by having wide thoughts, and much feeling for the rest of the world, as well as ourselves; and this sort of happiness often brings so much pain with it, that we can only tell it from pain by its being what we would choose before everything else, because our souls see it is good."